C150791301
D1180819

BRITAIN *in the* WILD

BRITAIN *in the* WILD

Jim Hallett

Weidenfeld and Nicolson
London

For Jack and Babette

Text and photographs © Jim Hallett 1993
Except for photographs pp.36, 37, 43 © Stuart Potter

First published in Great Britain in 1993 by
George Weidenfeld & Nicolson Limited
The Orion Publishing Group
Orion House, 5 Upper St Martin's Lane,
London WC2H 9EA

British Library Cataloguing in Publication Data
A catalogue for this book is available from the
British Library

0–297–83204–2

All rights reserved. No part of this publication
may be reproduced, stored in a retrieval system,
or transmitted in any form or by any means, electronic,
mechanical or otherwise, without the prior permission
of the copyright holder.

Designed by Joy FitzSimmons

Typeset by Deltatype Ltd, Ellesmere Port, Cheshire
Printed and bound in Italy

Illustrations
Half-title page: red squirrel
Frontispiece: lapwing chick hatching
Title page: greenfinch

KENT
ARTS & LIBRARIES
6150739323

C150 771 301

ACKNOWLEDGEMENTS

I would like to thank Jo Doyle for reading the text; Peter C. Hack for all his help in
Central Wales; Brian Johnson (English Nature) for his knowledge of the Somerset
Levels; Martin Noble (The Forestry Commission) for species identification and general
help in Lowland Heath; Alan and Heather Sangster for their moral support; Jonathan
Stacey (Scottish Natural Heritage) for help in locating upland species; and Doug Woods
for sharing his knowledge of dormice.

• CONTENTS •

INTRODUCTION

CRAYFISH

Though much smaller, crayfish are the freshwater equivalent of the lobster. When night falls, these aquatic crustaceans leave their daytime burrows to scavenge animal and vegetable detritus from the river bed. Today, crayfish are a fashionable delicacy, which has made crayfish farming a viable economic activity. This, in turn, has encouraged the importation of the larger, more commercially viable American signal crayfish for these farms. Unfortunately signal crayfish are an important vector in the spread of a fungal infection, *Aphanomyces astaci* or 'crayfish plague'. Though the imports are secured in 'ranches', inevitably crayfish and spores escape, contaminating rivers and streams. Recently Britain's native crayfish have disappeared from their favoured limestone and chalkland streams; in fact, they are absent from much of southern England.

'Where the bee sucks, there suck I
In a cowslip's bell I lie;
There I crouch when owls do cry.
On the bat's back I do fly
After summer merrily'
Ariel's Song (*The Tempest*)

BRITAIN PROVIDES A richness of flora and fauna that is hardly credible in such a small area. The waterfowl of wetland, the smooth snakes of sandy heath, the golden plover of tundra and the snowbunting of mountain top are just a few examples of this island's diverse wildlife and natural habitats.

Through the centuries man worked with Britain's climate soils and plants, taking enough for subsistence without seriously harming the environment. But such congeniality was not to last for ever. Today we are so out of tune with nature that Britain's natural riches have begun to slip through our fingers. Modern populations devour resources at an alarming rate, and satiating these vast appetites has drastic consequences. For example, our hunger for timber demands huge plantations that destroy unique upland habitats, while at sea level scarce lowland heath is sacrificed in the name of road transport. But it is the production of food that has wrought most change on the British countryside: to this end, we gave up our forest and hedgerows.

With these changes certain animals have become famous for their rarity. None but the most committed is likely to catch sight of the Dartford warbler or the otter. But now a second tier of British animals is disappearing. How many people can say they have seen a dormouse in the last fifteen years? How many small boys still fish for crayfish?

We all have a right to experience our heritage but, as valuable habitats disappear and memories fade, the alarming possibility is that future generations will get on with their lives unaware of the world's diminished quality and more accepting of future change.

To illustrate the vulnerability of our natural world I have explored six of Britain's most precious habitats – upland, montane, lowland heath, estuary, wetland and woodland – examining their history, their flora and fauna and the dangers that threaten them. In each case I have chosen one location that typifies each ecotype to examine it in more detail. I feel this practical explanation of an area's wildlife and conservation needs might make its beauty and significance more tangible – and its disappearance less acceptable.

Perceiving the need for conservation is, however, only the beginning. A host of practical problems must then be addressed. Who will pay? Should the farmer/property owner deprived of lucrative management practices accept his loss with good grace? Should all citizens that may benefit from a good environment pay towards some sort of compensation fund? If so, how large should this fund be?

A glance at the habitats featured in this book shows most of them to be transitional or artificial. British uplands and heathlands are to some extent man-made, while marshland and saltmarsh-estuary are unstable natural environments; even woodland may finally succumb to the deterioration of soils and grazing. So is the preservation of these places more than fashion?

In the first instance, halting natural transition only becomes necessary after habitats have been rescued from concrete and ploughs. Secondly, we have put such a huge spanner in the natural order of things that the process may no longer be in our best interests. Species that utilize more ephemeral habitats have survived this long because as one area ceased to provide for that species, so another began. However, habitats are now so restricted in Britain that this is no longer the case, making the management of what remains a necessity.

One of the key issues for British conservation is how great an area needs to be included in any protection programme, as a small area containing the species at risk often has complex relationships with the surrounding land. The only way to protect this land from the effects of encroaching developments is to create a buffer zone, such as a green belt. However, it is often hard to convince people of the far-reaching consequences of commercial enterprises when livelihoods are at stake. How we confront this dilemma reveals the resolution of our commitment to conservation.

It is important that this commitment is instilled soon. In the past much conservation energy grew from disenchantment with destruction. But, today, conservation must arise from an active appreciation of the importance of wildlife in our lives.

LESSER HORSESHOE BAT

The lesser horseshoe bat is now confined to south-west England and Wales. As natural tree roosts have disappeared, this species has turned to buildings for breeding and winter shelter. Man-made roosts are extremely vulnerable to a cycle of renovation, decay, and all the disturbance associated with close proximity to man. This, and associated loss of habitat, has resulted in an estimated decline of 97% for this species. Summer breeding colonies are typically found in large roof spaces and barns with free access, preferably adjacent to deciduous

woodland. Winter hibernation takes place in caves, mines, cellars and ice houses. Breeding begins in autumn, with copulation occurring throughout hibernation. Females can store sperm, allowing ovulation and fertilization to take place in spring. Females then gather in the nursery roost, where a single young is born around mid-July; by mid-August, young are independent. Unlike other species, greater and lesser horseshoe bats use the nose for echo-location (other species vocalise through their mouths).

• UPLAND •

GLENCOE
A macro perspective on the
work of the Ice Age is given by
Glencoe's classic 'U'-shaped
valley. During the Ice Age the
weight of continual snowfall
in the mountains pushed
glaciers through river valleys.
Boulders trapped in the ice
scraped the sides of the valley
until the characteristic 'U'
shape was achieved.

THE UPLANDS OF Britain can be divided into two regions: the true montane habitats lying over 2,000 feet and the submontane region of heather moor and acid grassland. In this chapter, we will be concerned with the latter. To understand the ecological importance of these areas we must examine how and when they were made. The extent to which submontane grasslands are man-made has, for example, been used by some as argument against their preservation. The landscape of both these regions is characterized by constant change. Climate, ecology and geology have all played a part in their transition towards the final climax vegetation of bog and peatland; but the hand of man has also shaped them, sometimes by design and sometimes through the unplanned consequences of his actions.

Upland history can be accurately reconstructed using recent scientific advances in pollen analysis. If you were to cut a deep trench and scan from the surface soil to the bottom, each layer would take you further back in geological time. The pollen still present in each of these layers tells us what plants were flowering in each period, and if something is known of the plants' ecology then deductions can be made concerning the climate and even the geography of the time.

We begin around 12350 BC, as the glaciers of northern Britain were melting. Pollen from this period reveals a rich mixture of herbaceous tundra and flowering plants: sea buckthorn, dwarf birch, willow, juniper and the flowers of rock rose, meadow rue and meadow sweet would have swayed in the Boreal wind. As the temperature climbed, birch colonized the valleys but arctic tundra was the dominant flora. On the ice's last retreat, about 6,600 years ago, air warmer than today's swept over Britain banishing all arctic plants to the mountain tops that still play host to them. Orbital changes had triggered an alteration in Britain's climate. For trees this meant a viable growing period right up to 2,500 feet, leaving only Britain's highest peaks showing through a green blanket of woodland. First to colonize were birch and pine, but hazel oak and alder followed. The age of the great British wildwood had begun.

Today's natural tree line is about 2,000 feet, though in reality trees are seldom found over 1,500 feet. The zone between the natural tree line and enclosed farmland or pasture is what is generally called 'uplands'. It is characterized by windswept heather moor or sheepwalks. The high trees of post-glacial Britain have gone, though anyone familiar with this landscape will have seen the bleached remains of pines that proclaim its woodland past. But what happened to the forests?

As has previously been said, the transition from woodland to moorland or bog is an interplay between climate, ecology and man. For ease of description I will treat these factors separately.

The deforestation of the north-west Highlands and Ireland is due primarily to climate. Since the time of blanket wildwood our seasons have become much damper. As centuries of rain percolated through young soils, minerals derived from the parent rock were leached from the surface leaving the top layers devoid of lime. While this was happening, clay particles flushed from above started to form a watertight barrier below the surface. Eventually large areas of upland become waterlogged, and soil organisms responsible for the breakdown of vegetable matter were deprived of oxygen. Thus the nutrients of dead plants remained locked in the plant structure forming peat, a nutrient-poor acid soil that inhibited most tree seedlings. As the peat layer thickened, tree seedlings could not reach through both peat and leached soils to the minerals they needed. Gradually the mature trees died and the forest with them, leaving heather to colonize the poor acid soils, and bogs to form in the hollows.

The first sign of human influence was Mesolithic man's burning of woodland to create pasture for the herbivores he hunted. Neolithic man after him (3000 years BC) was more sedentary and took to raising his own herbivores. The more man depended on his stock, the greater influence he exerted on the environment to make that husbandry successful. At first woodland was changed to open woodland. As enclosed pastures were a thing of the future, stock of this period needed to be of a kind that could defend itself, for example cattle and swine. But as wolves and other predators were eliminated, defenceless animals such as sheep could be safely grazed. For animal husbandry, forest clearance was expedient on two counts: it eradicated predators by destroying their habitat, and at the same time created new pasture. Within these areas of pasture, recolonization by forest was suppressed by grazing and periodic burning.

Much of upland Britain's moorland was, however, produced by the interaction of both human and natural agencies. As the forest was cleared from the drier slopes the increased runoff accelerated leaching and soil erosion, producing poor soils. The act of burning woodland also clogged water channels in the soil, accelerating the formation of bogs.

The upshot of all this activity was that species previously restricted in terms of ecological niches were presented with a host of new opportunities. Birds of the open forest or natural peat bog could adapt, and whole new biotic communities (unique to Great Britain) developed. Red grouse, merlin, hen harrier, short-eared owl, golden plover, ring ouzal and stonechat mixed with golden eagle, greenshank and black-throated diver in more northerly climes, while raven, peregrine and buzzard dominated the high sheepwalks.

Ironically these areas, many of which are man-made, are considered some of the last wild places in Britain. It is here that birds of prey and wading birds like golden plover, red grouse, peregine and golden eagle find their safest foothold, not only in Britain but in the whole of Europe.

But over the last one hundred years changes in the way man uses moorland has made the whole ecosystem unstable. Most moorland was originally managed as rough sheep pasture. Unfortunately the importance of heather as fodder has been in decline for centuries. Modern livestock is either wintered in the lowlands or given additional feed. This creates excessive grazing pressure on the heather in the summer, destroying the ecology of the hill.

The process is something like this. Heather like most woody plants grows at the tip, while grasses have their growing area well protected near or below ground level. If moors are overgrazed the heather cannot regenerate fast enough to combat the better graze-adapted grasses. The result is a steady change from species-rich heather to poor acid grasslands. The sheepwalks of Eskdale or the hills around Penrith are undoubtedly beautiful to look at, but they could never support the wildlife densities they once did. Overburning (burning heather can encourage new growth) all too often has the same effect by killing the vulnerable growing shoots. There is nothing new in this process – the Cistercian order had reduced the Pennines to acid grassland by 1550 – but modern-day subsidies based on headage payments have encouraged overgrazing on a much wider scale.

While sheep are exerting pressure on the high moorland, the lower slopes have been prey to the encroachment of more intensive farming. Even in my lifetime the loss of Exmoor to plough and pasture has graphically illustrated improved farming techniques.

The saving grace for moorland ecosystems has been the vested interest of the sportsman. This reached its peak with the Victorian propensity to spend its vast excess income on shooting and hunting in Scotland. In fact most contemporary heather moor owes it existence to the revenue supplied by grouse and deer sport. Today, however, there is a new threat that plans to sweep all before it. In recent years great phalanxes of exotic conifer plantations have been imposed on our uplands – 2½ million acres since 1940. The predators they harbour reduce the red grouse and, as the annual bag falls, the sporting rates look less of a bargain than the subsidized returns (up to 70% of the costs) on forestry. So the inexorable pine blanket spreads.

This bears no comparison to the open mixed woodland of the wildwood. Close planting ensures that the trees only have room to grow directly skyward, without shoulder room for branches other than the sun-tight canopy. Below, in the darkness, pine needles create a soil so acid that its runoff poisons the streams, stopping the aquatic dipper breeding and disrupting salmon and trout. The deep ploughing preparation for planting of these 'woodlands' so erodes the fragile upland soils that a twenty-fold increase in runoff clogs rivers and the fragile hydrology of bog systems. The impossibility of burning close to forest has also led to a deterioration of the adjacent moorland.

For ground-nesting birds the disruption is immense and apart from the direct loss of habitat there are knock-on effects. For example, many birds of the open moor have regular mates and breeding areas (greenshank even use the same nest scrape) and disruption or displacement so confuses pairs that they lose each other. Even if displaced birds find long-standing mates, their lack of local knowledge can lead to breeding failure. Worse still, their movement to other areas can stretch the limited resources of this ecosystem to the extent that both new and resident birds fail to breed.

Though this business has caused the fastest declines in species associated with peat bog, like snipe and golden plover, all sorts of species are affected. In the south of Scotland a study of ravens in a particular area revealed that occupancy of traditional nesting sites dropped by 72% between 1960 and 1981. Claims are often made that the large birds of prey can make use of these woods, but the truth is often more complicated. For example, a study of four pairs of golden eagle in south-west Scotland revealed that two pairs had stopped breeding when large-scale forestry encroached on their range. It seems that prior to breeding, eagles like to prey on large ground-nesting birds such as grouse, the very birds displaced by afforestation.

Effects like these are more insidious when they take place in as upland of true international importance, but this is what has been happening in the 'Flow Country' of Caithness.

THE FLOW COUNTRY

The Flow Country is not particularly high, but in ecological terms it is the quintessential upland community. Though the area is nearly always described as desolate and inhospitable my most vivid recollections are how the emerald green sphagnum mounds, studded with lichens and heather, mushroomed from the dark peaty water. In spells of sunshine, the rich greens of moss and the reds of heather contrast with the delicate florets of lichens, looking for all the world like sumptuous cushions.

DAWN OVER THE NORTH-WEST COAST OF SCOTLAND
The consistently high rainfall in the north-west Highlands brought about a natural deforestation, allowing upland plant communities to meet the sea.

The mire system of the Flows is the one terrestrial habitat seen better in Britain than anywhere else. You may go to Austrialia for coral reefs or to Poland for ancient deciduous woodland, but for rolling moorland Britain is best. This is an area of international significance, judged by an international panel of mire specialists to be on a par with the Serengeti in terms of ecological interest. The cool damp oceanic climate and undulating topography of northern Scotland create some of the most favourable conditions for bog development in the world. This area has the greatest expanse of blanket bog in the Northern hemisphere; a fact made more important by the realization that only 13% of the world's mire systems have survived.

In 1987 the then Nature Conservancy Council (NCC), recognizing these facts, carried out a survey of the topography, ornithology and plant life of the Caithness and Sutherland flows. The resulting report states that its unique quality comes from northerly ecosystems in such a southerly position. This has produced a variety of bogs that exist in no other place in the world. Of the fifteen types the NCC specify as worthy of note, the most important are as follows: there are bogs with drainage systems that change as the level of peat rises; bogs that are important for certain species like cranberry; bogs that maintain soft quaking mire; bogs that are patterned with pools; bogs where pools are covered with sphagnum; bogs characterized by certain species like dwarf birch; and deep-peat tundra bogs found nowhere else in the world. The overriding theme of the report is the sheer diversity of forms to be found in these areas.

On ornithology the report found waders in 'outstanding overall numbers and diversity, and the occurrence of at least 15 breeding species reflects the variety of peatland and open water habitat'. There is in fact a wider ecological spectrum of breeding here than in any other moorland area in Britain. Many of the species rely on naturally treeless open wetlands and tundra, and though this habitat is simulated elsewhere in Britain, nowhere is it quite the same. Within the British Isles as a whole, rolling moorland apes vegetation types generally found further north, thereby attracting northerly species of birds to mix with those of the south. But the conjunction of natural moorland with true tundra affinities in the Flows produces a precise combination of species not represented anywhere else in the world.

Apart from rare communities of birds, rare species are also well represented. Temmerick, stint, ruff, wood sandpiper, hen harrier and arctic skua are but a few examples.

Despite all this, afforestation is permitted to threaten the Flow Country. The advances in deep ploughing and the propagation of seedlings have made previously unplantable areas vulnerable. With this new technology blanket peat of more than one and a half feet deep is seen as suitable. Foresters argue that they are returning the landscape to a more natural form, but the climate of the Flows has never allowed dense forest, as proved by the failure of these forests to withstand the 1987 gales. The effect of this industry can be gauged by noting the changes in the population of certain key species. Though not particularly rare, the affinity of golden plover, dunlin and greenshank for quality peatland makes them excellent indicator species. Golden plover have an affinity for the eroded hags, and dunlin are attracted to the wet areas, while greenshank nest in both locations. An investigation into their progress would reflect the changes in the area as a whole. These species can also be used to illustrate how reliant global populations are on this one area. It is estimated that 17% of the European community's (EC) golden plover breed here, 35% (EC) of dunlin and 100% (EC) of greenshank.

In 1987 it was estimated that 19% of golden plover pairs, 17% of dunlin pairs and 17% of greenshank pairs had already been lost to afforestation. This figure excludes those lost indirectly through increased predation and breeding disruption as described above. From these declines we can assume that the internationally significant populations of red throated diver (14% EC), black throated diver (20% EC), graylag goose (43% EC), and widgeon (20% EC) have also been affected.

So what should be done to save this area? The report of 1989 discovered many areas and species that warrant protection. At present, criteria for conservation involve the plotting of species in a particular area and the subsequent protection of that area. But the forces that shape the Flow Country are on such a large scale that this approach will not work. At its most basic, the Flow Country is a result of the water cycle, and to protect the ecosystem this cycle must be preserved. Weather systems of the Atlantic yield their moisture to the mountains of Sutherland, fuelling hydrology systems throughout the area. This water is the life's blood of the system but its journey from mountain top to sea is too complex for anyone to know. En route it may move through *dubh lochain* (black lochs), quaking mire, sphagnum-filled pools and other unique features. Interference with its flow at any stage, by afforestation for example, threatens subsequent habitats. If we do not recognize this interdependence with blanket protection then legal, piecemeal destruction will render conservation irrelevant. As it is, this piecemeal destruction proceeded at a pace of 123 acres a week in 1989 and 17% already under afforestation. I will leave the last word to D. A. Ratcliffe, Chief Scientist of the NCC until 1989:

The ecosystem is more than the sum of its parts. The ecosystem represents the totality of nature in the functional interdependence of the many physical and biological components and the complexity of their relationships. The ecosystem should thus be the basis of conservation concern.

UPLAND BLANKET BOGS

Though there are pools present, the eastern Highlands (right) is a much drier area than the Flows (left); there are more lichens and fewer mosses. In the gullies, the hoary and bleached remains of pines have been uncovered by fast-flowing winter streams. Golden plovers and oystercatchers breed on higher, heather-dominated areas, while snipe favour the damper sections. In the Flow Country of Caithness (left) the scene is altogether more lush and the water courses in

this upland mire seem to defy gravity. The ground falls away in all directions from this point, but the peat retains enough water to fill these pools. On the ridges between them, arctic birch and other tundra plants bear witness to the inhospitable climate, while the active sphagnum beds indicate the high rainfall. Though there are only about 150 miles between these two pictures, the climate of the eastern highlands is decidedly more Continental than that of Caithness.

DIPPER

Common to many aquatic
animals, the dipper's breeding
season begins early: February
in exceptional years, though
March is more common.
This is because aquatic
environments are less affected
by the harshness of winter,
and the dipper's prey items
(aquatic invertebrates) are
present early in the year. The
wren-like domed nest is built
by both sexes, often behind
waterfalls or some other site
overlooking water. Five eggs
are incubated by the female
alone for fifteen to eighteen
days. The nestlings are fed by
both parents for a further
three weeks. In the Highlands
the acid runoff from forestry
plantations is killing the
aquatic insects and
crustaceans that support this
bird. Further down the water
course pollution is having the
same effect.

RAVENS

The raven's breeding season
usually begins in March,
though on Cornish cliffs
February is not unknown.
These birds pair for life, and
may bond before they are
mature enough to breed. This
stability is further evidenced
in nest building: once a
breeding territory has been
established they build the one
nest that should suffice for the
rest of their lives. Each year
the female will incubate four
to six eggs for about twenty
days. The young are tended
by both parents for a further
five to six weeks. These ravens
were photographed in the
Elan Valley, Wales, an area
reputed to support the second
most dense population of
these birds in the world. This
is a sheep-rearing area and the
afterbirth of lambing is an
important source of food.
Other prey items include
small mammals and birds as
well as plants.

RED GROUSE

Wholly dependent on young shoots of heather, the red grouse follows this plant from sea-level to the lower boundaries of the ptarmigan. Males choose territories in August and hold them till the following spring. Within these areas sexual displays begin in February and continue until cocks attract a mate. In May the acquired female will dig the nest scrape and lay an average of seven to eight eggs. The twenty-eight days' incubation is completed by the female alone, with the male in close attendance. The maintenance of grousemoor through the persecution of upland predators has brought mammals like wild cat, and many birds of prey, to the point of extinction in Britain. Against this loss must be weighed the preservation of British upland moors for many species. Despite all this, red grouse numbers have fallen drastically and specific shoots are very restricted. With this decline, farming and forestry have usurped moorland.

GOLDEN PLOVER

If red grouse are important for the preservation of uplands, then golden plover are equally important as an indicator of this habitat's condition. Because of this, declines associated with the loss of habitat to farming and afforestation are worrying. In general, golden plover breed in peaty heathland and bog from 800 to 2,000 feet. Flocks arrive at their breeding sites in early spring, the males establishing the territories they hope to breed in. They can be seen song-flighting from February to July, circling with slow, deliberate wing beats, or executing spectacular dives. Once paired, three to four eggs are laid in a shallow scrape in mid-April. Both sexes incubate for twenty-seven days, and chicks are mobile soon after hatching. This one is nestling among peat sods cut for household use by the landowner. The lighter face denotes a southern variant of the species.

COMMON BUZZARD

This species was in the vanguard of recovery from DDT insecticide poisoning; a remarkable achievement considering this period saw myxomatosis decimate their principal food source, the rabbit. Upland populations, that escaped the worst excesses of gamekeepers, acted as a reservoir from which the lowlands were recolonized. Although they might take a few grouse chicks, mammals are the largest element in their diet. The nest is a bulky structure that may be used for many seasons. In late March or early April three to four eggs are laid and incubated by the female, though the male may help. Incubation may last between thirty-three days for single eggs and forty-two for a clutch. For the first ten days after hatching the male hunts while the female closely tends the chicks; later both parents hunt. Except in very good years, the smallest chick usually dies. This chick was photographed in the Elan Valley, central Wales.

FEMALE REDSTART

This summer visitor from sub-Saharan Africa has been subject to the same population fluctuation as the whitethroat, and suffered the same decline in 1969 (see page 113). Redstarts are typically found in highland scrub woods and stone-wall country, but reach their highest densities in sessile oak. As well as tree stumps they will nest in rock crevices and holes in walls. In early May a loosely constructed cup of grass, lined with wool and feathers, is built by the female. She also incubates the six to seven eggs unaided. In two weeks the eggs hatch and the male helps during the fifteen-day nestling period. This picture was taken in sessile oakwoods managed by the RSPB. The nest site was typically on the upper limit of the wood.

ARCTIC BIRCH

Many species of plant exhibit dwarfism in harsh climatic conditions: pines can grow no higher than seedlings in the Cairngorms, and in the Flow Country the birch family produces this dwarf birch. Its location is an indication of a highly restricted climatic condition, thus conservationists use it as a bench-mark in the assessment of an area's likely ecological importance. On an international scale it is a circumpolar plant associated with Arctic tundra, and in Britain it is a Caithness and Sutherland speciality.

MOORLANDS OF DORBACK BURN BY ABERNETHY FOREST

There is ample evidence that hill peatlands were once afforested. In some cases deforestation followed a natural change in climate, but in the eastern Highlands the hand of man has shaped the countryside. Certainly much of the Caledonian wildwood was sold to English ironmasters after the failure of the 1745 Jacobite Rebellion. This blanket peat was photographed in the eastern Highlands. Sphagnum, the raw material of peat, has long since died here, leaving acid grasses to dominate; note also the invasion of birch in the background.

GLACIAL EROSION

As ice moved over the
Highlands, rocks embedded
in the glacier scraped deep
scars in the bedrock. Evidence
of this violence is usually
buried under layers of soft
peat, but it is visible on some
rocky outcrops in Sutherland.
Here, mosses, lichens and
heather try to gain a foothold
where detritus has become
trapped in the striations.

THE RUGGED VIEWS OF SUTHERLAND

On the gentle slopes of the
foreground, blanket peat has
created boggy acid grass and
heather sheep graze. In the
midground the hillocks are
too steep to allow peat
formation and the glacial
scraped rock still shows
through the thin soil. In the
background is the bare peak
of Stac Polly.

• MONTANE •

THE PLATEAU

The view from the summit of Cairn Gorm (4,084 feet), across to the peaks of Beinn Mheadhoin and Ben Macdui and the frozen Loch Etchachan. Just beyond the Cairn Gorm scree plateau, in the foreground, a ravine plunges 2,000 feet to Loch Avon and just as abruptly rises to the opposite peaks. Despite these deep erosions the surface area of the summit is large enough to support an arctic ecosystem left marooned by the retreating Ice Age. Until the 1920s there were snow beds that had never thawed in living memory. Today, with fears of global warming, these vestigial glacial habitats are very vulnerable.

THE HARSHNESS OF true montane regions gives rise to a sparse ecology that must eke a living from thin soils. Low temperatures inhibit any chemical maturation of these soils, keeping their chemistry similar to that of the parent rock. These are soils in their infancy, waiting to creep down the mountainside and mature in more hospitable surroundings. In plateau regions thicker soil layers are often buried beneath rock detritus extruded by frost action, creating a chaotic landscape of ice, wind and bare rock. More than any other habitat, montane areas are characterized by change and development.

To a large extent altitude has little effect on wildlife: the critical factor is temperature. A fall in temperature of about 1°F with every 300 foot rise causes high peaks to mimic habitats of more northerly regions. For instance at 2,000 feet the climate of the eastern Highlands resembles that of south Iceland at sea level. This mimicry is good enough to allow the same species to be found in both locations. In fact, throughout Europe arctic species inhabit higher altitudes as they move south, with ptarmigan breeding at sea level in Greenland, at 3,280 feet in Great Britain, and at 6,562 feet in the Alps. The prevailing weather systems also have a bearing on the distribution of species. For example, most plants have a minimum growing temperature. While this temperature may be reached for eight months of the year at sea level, the nearby 3,280 foot peak's climate will be 10°F lower, rendering the growing season too brief to complete the reproductive cycle of many plants. Because of this, the length of the summer can restrict the height at which a plant can exist. Scotland's generally cool summers, for example, can restrict the viable growing altitude of Scots pine to approximately 2,296 feet; while in the Alps the warm summers lengthen the growing season, generally allowing the same species to reach an altitude of 5,577 feet.

Plants have devised certain modifications for montane regions: some dispense with sexual reproduction and grow clones in place of flowers, thus shortening the reproductive cycles. Where time is not at a premium, the most common adaptation is to avoid harsh weather and overwinter as seeds, but if this is not possible then starch reserves are converted to soluble sugar creating a sort of antifreeze that prevents the structure rupturing in freezing conditions.

Mammals and birds must also devise strategies against the cold. The adaptations of the mountain hare in comparison to the brown hare are indicative of most mammals. In winter a white thick coat is grown for insulation and camouflage. In many species, including the mountain hare, the feet are particularly well insulated to reduce heat loss through contact with the snow. Shorter ears reduce heat loss through wind chill as does the use of a burrow in poor weather. For ground-nesting birds, wind chill and camouflage are critical. To this end the ptarmigan loses the pure white plumage of winter to adopt the mottled appearance that blends perfectly with the mountain landscape. The dotterel's tendency to sit on eggs despite any interruption is a useful trait where eggs can chill so quickly.

One last feature common to the flora and fauna of these regions is their vulnerability to changes in the local environment. In many parts of the world these creatures can roam over large areas, but the montane specialists of Europe are often isolated, existing on the edge of viability.

THE CAIRNGORMS

My first views of the Cairngorms in the Scottish Highlands inspired suprise and wonder. The mountains in the western Highlands are spectacular, but the scale of the Cairngorm range renders it much more than an ostentatious feature in familiar surroundings: you feel as though you have entered an alien landscape.

Its remote splendour has moved writers and naturalists for years. More than a century ago John Hill Barton, a pioneer in the appreciation of the area, described it as follows:

> The depth and remoteness of solitude, the huge mural precipices, the deep chasms between the rocks, the waterfalls of unknown height, the hoary remains of primeval forest, the fields of eternal snow, and the deep black lakes at the foot of precipices are full of such associations of awe and grandeur and mystery as no other scenery in Britain is capable of arousing.

The granite massif of the Cairngorms was once part of a mountain range that stretched from Scotland to Scandinavia. While the remaining peaks, so close together and matched in height, betray a plateau origin, ice and snow, wind and water have cut and worn some of the most widespread landforms outside the Arctic. Views from the plateau summit reveal a vast area of frozen wilderness with rolling hills, granite tors, sheer-faced corries and frozen lochs – a landscape deserving of respect.

Anyone standing on the Cairngorms' summit would recognize an arctic influence in the plants and animals, but the moist air from the Atlantic also has a bearing, creating a unique system of arctic, oceanic and alpine communities. As with Caithness and Sutherland it is the size of the area that makes an ecosystem viable, creating the most important montane wildlife in the European community. From the late snow beds of Ben Macdui (4,691 feet), down to the Caledonian pinewoods around Loch Eilien (918 feet), the nature reserve is 'our foremost conservation area'. While the lower slopes are of great interest, they are outside the scope of this chapter (See Woodland). Here, we will limit ourselves to the alpine and summit ecologies.

This region starts at about 2,300 feet, where the heather becomes stunted and wind-flattened. At this height, birds of the lower slopes, such as golden plover, are still present, but the cushions of lichen intermixed in the heather show the growth of a montane influence. Alpine shrubs, such as bearberry, crowberry and least willow, anchor soils that would otherwise creep down the valley under the action of ice and water. Higher still, the snow lingers and the hardy blaeberry replaces heather as the dominant plant, interspersed with mosses and clubmosses. In the late snow beds, matt grass takes over from blaeberry.

Above 3,000 feet an almost constant wind prevents late snow cover and the soils are fragile. The constant erosion and runoff leave only young soils, still rich with the minerals of the parent rock but low in organic matter. As the base rock is weathered to gravel, colonizing mosses and lichens begin the process of humification. The dying mosses degenerate and raise the organic content of the soil, allowing grasses to gain a foothold. In the true montane habitats of the Cairngorms, the dominant three-pointed rush and moss campion are punctuated with areas of woolly hair moss and lichens. These form deep, greenish-grey carpets called rhacomitrium heath, the typical habitat of the dotterel, snowbunting and ptarmigan.

The wildlife of this rugged terrain could never rival lowland woodland for density, but there are more species than you might imagine. The area also boasts alpine/arctic specialists not found anywhere else in Britain. The plateau species of bird already mentioned create a great deal of interest, but a total of 136 species of bird have been recorded in the area.

The mammals have only one native montane specialist, the mountain hare, but the diversity of animals that visit the summit plateau is astonishing considering the weather. Common and pigmy shrews, and short-tailed voles provide prey for the foxes and stoats, while reindeer and red deer graze on the shrub and moss heaths. The late snow lie also produces a few specialist arctic insects.

These communities are relics of a bygone age, outposts of the Ice Age's retreat. Here, we can enjoy an ancient landscape with its specialist flora and fauna, but this is a fragile

CALEDONIAN COCCIFERA

This lichen becomes more prevalent with height. When it shares a summit with rhacomitrium heath it grows in dense patches, sometimes two feet square. The aspect of mosses and lichens, being dominant features of the vegetation, creates an alien appearance to those not familiar with these heights. The area seems both lush and barren at the same time.

ecosystem, always on the edge of sustainability. The underlying vulnerability of the Cairngorms is the confused bureaucratic situation. Fifteen different bodies and various private landowners exercise control in the area, and in the absence of an authoritative overview they each pursue their own interests. In the past these developments have been detrimental to the area's ecology.

A great threat is the development of skiing. The industry began in the late Forties and initially growth was slow, but the 'boom' years of the early Sixties saw a tenfold increase. Today there are four main ski resorts and six others are proposed, so the number of skiers rises annually. Compared to France or the USA Britain's skiing industry is small, but the oceanic influence in the weather forces development into very sensitive areas. In most continental ski resorts the snow lie lasts longer on lower parts of the mountain where soils are more stable. However, the search for late snow in British temperate zones takes skiers to much higher ground, resulting in frenetic activities in places that can least withstand it.

Unfortunately the highest plateaux with the most outstanding plants and animals adjoin the corries and slopes most coveted by the skiers. Damage is twofold. Initially there are the consequences of construction: pistes are gouged out of the mountainside with bulldozers, destroying a mountain flora that is unlikely to recover. A second phase of damage begins after the construction teams have left. We have seen in the previous chapter how the hydrology and runoff systems in uplands are extremely important. The crux of conservation in mountain areas is the protection of watersheds through the maintenance of the fragile carpet of plants. When these plants are eroded and the shape of the hill is modified by bulldozers, these watersheds quickly crumble. The disruption to natural runoff patterns has dire consequences, which Scotland has already experienced. In the Cairn Gorm and Glen Shee areas, the increased runoff has caused considerable widening of the waterways and the wholesale slumping of hillsides. Sand and gravel have been taken from areas where rare plants were established and dumped over areas that may be just as valuable. Even footpaths can become conduits in times of high rainfall, disrupting the natural direction of the water away from areas that rely on it (there is no hope for areas of bog that relied on the original water supply). As the protective layer of vegetation is lost, more soil is eroded and areas that once soaked up excessive rain and snow melt become fast conductors of water. Consequently, flash floods in the valleys have been a problem in skiing areas in the Cairngorms.

A more direct effect of skiing is the deliberate movement of snow to extend the season. Late snow lie is a rare ecotype in Great Britain and its artificial production to extend the skiing season suppresses the natural fauna of the area.

MOUNTAIN HARE

The mountain hare is a creature of tundra and Boreal forest zones. On continental mountain ranges it is rarely seen below 4,265 feet, though it occurs on lower slopes in Britain. Its natural home here is the highlands of Scotland and Ireland, but it has also been introduced to the Lake District, the Pennines and the Peak District. Seen here in its winter coat, it is easy to distinguish it from the brown hare, but as spring progresses the mountain hare's white camouflage turns grey, so its shorter ears are then the best clue. Unlike the brown hares, the mountain species digs shallow burrows in the summer that leverets will use if chased, but young are always born above ground (three litters each season). Most leverets are taken by foxes, and buzzards; wild cats and golden eagles also take adults.

Ramblers and hikers are additional threats, especially to lichens, and 600 miles of new tracks now take them to previously unspoilt areas. Vegetation and soil erosion were already severe in the late 1960s, but today features of degradation, long apparent on the ski slopes, are appearing on the plateau itself. At the most-popular sites, litter and foodscraps are supporting such high densities of crows and gulls that the ground-nesting birds no longer breed there.

There are other threats to the area aside from recreational interests. The granite rocks that form the massif produce a poor acid soil that has traditionally dissuaded grazing. But the recent trends in intensive stocking plus the perennial problem of red deer are taking their toll. Under pressure from grazing, moss heath has given way to sheep's fescue or other grasses and rushes. The decline of rhacomitrium heath is all but complete in England and Wales. Many Welsh uplands have been reduced to bare rock, while most northerly hills in England have become grasslands, pushing ptarmigan and dotterel ever further north.

Whether the birds and mammals of the high mountain tops will continue to find a home on the schist massif of the Cairngorms is hard to tell. Recent management decisions sympathetic to conservation were enforced by a groundswell of popular support, but if enthusiasm for the wildlife of the area wanes it is hard to see how the area could resist the economic pressures of tourism.

SNOW BUNTING

Britain's small breeding population of snow buntings is swelled annually with birds wintering along the east coast. If the continental winter is severe, the visitors may penetrate much further west. In Great Britain the snow bunting mostly breeds in the north-east Highlands, where it joins the ptarmigan and dotterel in a trio of specialist montane birds. It generally survives on a diet of rush seeds and lichens, but it seems that the insects associated with late snow lie may also be important to this species during the breeding season. The season begins in late May when a cup of grasses and occasional ptarmigan feathers is constructed, hidden among rocks and scree. The female incubates the four to six eggs for about two weeks. She then broods them for a further five days while the male feeds both her and the chicks. Later both birds tend the young.

RHACOMITRIUM HEATH

The biological history of this heathland begins with the colonization of bare rock by pioneerng mosses. As portions of these matts are torn by wind and grazing, the dying mosses add vegetable matter to the thin soils, creating humus. Sedges colonize this improved earth, and, with the addition of lichens, the rhacomitrium heath community is complete. Once present throughout the Pennines and the mountains of Wales it has been destroyed by overgrazing and trampling. Today it is largely confined to the mountains of Scotland and even here the weight of tourism has taken its toll. The consequence of this deterioration is the restriction of our alpine/arctic breeding birds that rely on it, such as the ptarmigan and dotterel.

ALPINE CLUBMOSS

On the hills of Wales, the northern Pennines and the Malverns, the alpine clubmoss is a frequent member of dwarf shrub communities between 1,500 and 4,000 feet. Here, they have proved extremely vulnerable to grassland improvement and afforestation. In the Cairngorms this extremely hardy plant is associated with late snow lie ecosystems that also include bilberry, sedges and Caledonian lichens. These fronds are visible from August to September.

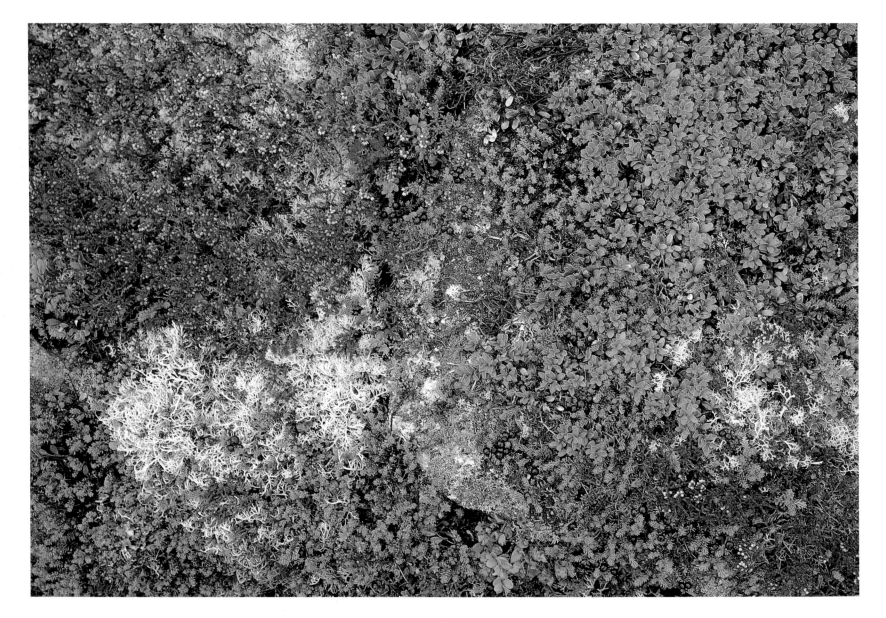

PROSTRATE HEATHS ON CARN BÀN MOR

At 700 metres crowberry and cowberry form dense and prostrate mats. In autumn the fruits of these plants are very important for ptarmigan and the caterpillars of montane moths such as the black mountain and mountain burnet. The cowberry has small white or pink flowers from May to July, while the crowberry's pink flowers last from April to June.

MITOPUS MARIO

This creature is not a spider but part of the order of harvestmen. These differ from spiders in having no waist: the head, chest and abdomen are compressed into one block. Lacking spinnerets they cannot trap prey in webs and so rely on hunting and scavenging. To this end, harvestmen have been observed imprisoning prey in a palisade of legs, and dropping on them from above. This particular specimen is *Mitopus mario*, and while the sub-species *Mitopus alpinus* has been proposed it has yet to be acknowledged. The creature was photographed at an altitude of 3,641 feet, hunting by day during a snow storm, none of which is characteristic of *Mitopus mario*. The mating of this species has no ceremony, and copulation is the last act of males; females may survive long enough to lay two batches of eggs.

PTARMIGAN

These ground-nesting birds use arctic tundra as red grouse use heather. They consume prostrate montane plants – crowberry and blaeberry – and Caledonian lichens and mosses. In the cool climes of the Flow Country they can be found as low as 600 feet, though around 2,000 feet is their usual lower limit in Britain. They are restricted in this country as conical hills present such limited areas between 2,000 and 3,800 feet. The Cairngorm plateau is one of the few areas that fulfils the ptarmigan's requirements in this respect. It struts over the surface with great deliberation, never taking flight until forced to, preferring a controlled scuttle. In such a featureless environment, this lack of movement makes it very difficult to spot and this allied to seasonally adapted camouflage is its defence strategy. This cock was photographed in April, shortly before the breeding season.

DOTTEREL

R. Kearton in *British Birds Nests*, 1895, informs us that the dotterel was mostly absent from the hills of England by 1895. This was almost certainly due to the loss of moss heathland. Like the ptarmigan, this summer visitor is really a bird of the tundra; its breeding in Britain is largely limited to Scottish peaks, with small populations in the Lake District. In late May an average of three eggs are laid in a shallow scrape in the tundra. These are incubated by the male for twenty-five days, and subsequently tended by him for a further four weeks. The reluctance of the male to leave the nest when approached made it literally a sitting target for those that habitually hunted it in the past for its plumage (much prized by fly fishermen) and accorded it local names such as 'foolish dotterel'.

• Lowland Heath •

The New Forest Heaths

A mist clings to the lowland bogs of Vales Moor in the New Forest. This view from Castle Hill over the heaths and bogs of Crainsmoor shows the encroachment of Bournemouth in the distance. Ridges of red heath and tumuli stand above the swards of molinia bog, creating soil dry enough to sustain the scattered pines. The intervening bogs are rich in plants exploiting the southerly location.

It may seem a touch esoteric to maintain any distinction between moorland and heath. The standard definition of heathland as 'an area where heather or some form of the *Ericaceae* is usually the dominant form of vegetation' is not helpful, and the assertion that 'heaths are of drier sandy-clay soils while moors are products of older rocks with high rainfall and lower average temperatures' is useful but misses the essential feature. For many people the true distinction is one of ecology. At their best, lowland heaths are a rich mixture of heathers, wetlands, stands of gorse and different forms of grassland.

Unfortunately this habitat's rich diversity is matched by its scarcity, making the animals and plants that rely on it some of the most endangered species in the British Isles. Sand lizards, smooth snakes and Dartford warblers are all largely confined to the southernmost counties that maintain this habitat.

On an international scale the large European heaths have all but disappeared, though fine examples persisted until late into the last century. Their growth and subsequent decline is interwoven with the social evolution of Europe in much the same way as that of British uplands.

It is generally assumed that the great clearance of heaths took place in Neolithic times as man created farmland from wildwood. His Mesolithic predecessor was thought to be a simple hunter-gatherer confined to coastal areas and the borders of lakes. However, recent excavations of Mesolithic tumuli within heaths indicate that his practice of burning woodland to encourage game (see Upland) was difficult to control in the dry climate associated with lowland heaths. By the time the farms of Neolithic man expanded beyond the fertile wetlands, the southern heaths would not have presented the inpenetrable wildwood one might have imagined.

Uncontrolled Mesolithic burning was the first stage in the destruction of naturally poor soils. As fires raged, precious nutrients were lost in smoke, and ash was drained away with rainwater. The secondary growth that thrived in this impoverished environment was even more susceptible to fire, and so a vicious circle was created. When Neolithic man began farming on these slopes the soil was already depleted. The trees that had reached deep into the earth and brought goodness to the surface soils of the wildwood were gone, and arable farming finally exhausted what remained. As the soil deteriorated, acid-tolerant plants such as calluna and erica began to dominate, smothering most other species and creating an inhospitable seed bed with their leaf litter. By the end of the Bronze Age these areas had been reduced to sheep browse.

The decline of heathland has its roots in changes in society. Historically heaths have been subject to a fairly intensive land use. As well as grazing, they provided pastoral communities with peat and wood for fuel, heather for thatch, bracken for bedding and litter, and various berries for food. However, as these communities died, their land management techniques died with them. Straw replaced bracken, and the use of fodder for winter feed made the calluna superfluous. In Europe the advent of cheap wool from Australia destroyed the economy of the heathland flocks, while the increased agricultural efficiency on more fertile soils (in particular, the increase in dairy produce) meant that heathland farms could not compete. Without grazing or burning, seedlings of pine and birch took root, and abandoned heath returned to scrub and then woodland. All over Europe farmers saw economic sense in turning heathland over to the timber production that was its ecological niche and restricting farming to those soils that suited cultivation. The decline was dramatic: heathland shrank from 75% of non-cultivated land to 5%.

The British decline was no less severe. Between 1800 and 1983, 75% of lowland heath was destroyed. Most was converted to pasture or arable farming, but much was lost to urban development. In the magazine *Science Gossip*, the Bournemouth of 1868 was described as a 'small village surrounded by large expanses of moorland . . . [on which] *Coronella austriaca* [smooth snake] was extraordinarily abundant'. Today that heath is below the suburbs of Bournemouth and Poole, and the little that remains is always under pressure from urban expansion. Where heaths have been preserved, their proximity to urban populations make summer fires wholesale killers of the slow-moving animals such as sand lizards, smooth snakes and Dartford warbler chicks.

Though many heaths are now protected from farming or building, the social function that created them is missing. Perhaps the most important feature of the old management system is grazing. Without it, heaths are drowned in seas of purple moor grass and wavy hair grass. The most celebrated example of successful heathland management in Britain today are the New Forest heaths of Hampshire.

THE NEW FOREST

The New Forest itself has an anachronistic air about it. Leaving the main road and crossing the first cattle grid takes you into mature beechwoods with closely grazed lawns. The New Forest ponies are languid in the heat of summer and speed limitations on the intrusive motor car ensure their peace is not disturbed. Here the ponies, donkeys and

KEELED SKIMMER

With a characteristic low, fast flight skimmers seem to glide over the peaty bogs of the forest, congregating in areas of open water. The males continually patrol their bog or stream, pouncing on females and dragging them to the centre of their territory. After mating, the pair fly in tandem, hovering over the water as the female deposits eggs by flicking the water's surface with her abdomen. Skimmers are on the wing from May to September. The larvae inhabit the streams and ponds of wetlands for two years.

other grazers always have right of way. Outside the woodlands the heaths seem to contradict the obvious signs of intensive urban development. They could not be described as beautiful in the way that the Highlands are: the horizon reveals roads or telegraph poles rather than mountain ranges.

The New Forest comprises a bewildering number of habitats. Grassland gives way to bogs containing all three species of sundews, marsh gentians and bog asphodel; bog crickets and a host of dragonflies abound, along with snipe and their chicks. The gentle slopes of the heathland, crowned with dry heath, hide the rare smooth snake and sand lizard, but silver studded blue and grayling butterflies are easy to spot as they feed from the heather. And all around there is the oak woodland.

This mosaic of habitats is the result of a complex geological history. Generally speaking the southern heaths are on sedimentary rocks deposited by the frequent encroachment of the sea, while northern soils were laid down by rivers and streams fed by the meltwater of the great northern ice sheet. But subsequent erosion and deposition have masked this picture, creating a mixture throughout the area.

The area's social history is just as important. Like most heaths it owes its initial escape from agricultural exploitation to its poor soils. The chalk soils of the south of the region have seen what agricultural development there has been, while the poorer soils of the north have escaped all recent farming. The most important ecological event in the forest's social history was its appropriation by the Crown in 1069 to make it a Royal Forest. Though his afforestation did not involve any change of ownership, strict rules of land management were imposed. For centuries the utilization of the heaths for grazing, fuel, bedding and food had been uncontrolled, but under the Crown all this would be strictly audited. Initially the most important change was the outlawing of enclosure or cultivation within the 'perambulation', and the Crown's reserving of all rights to take game. This protected the existing forest from exploitation by advances in agriculture, but at the same time ensured enough deer persisted to stop forest regeneration on existing heath. Rights to use the heath in a traditional manner were accorded to those owning land within the forest, but care was taken to ensure this did not interfere with the ecology of the area. The whole system was overseen by the stewards through a yearly cycle, and the number of beasts each commoner was allowed to graze was limited to the amount of stock the land could sustain in winter. If this type of management had lasted until today, the upland sheepwalks might still be rolling heathermoor.

Apart from grazing, the most ecologically important activity was probably turf-cutting. In days before motor transport, the movement of fuel must have been an arduous business, and so the opportunity to cut one's own peat fuel close to the house was a godsend. From the detailed accounts of Colin Tubbs (NCC Senior Officer for the Isle of Wight for thirty years) it seems that the peaty wet soils were those most sought after. If the customary 'cut one and leave two' practice was observed, 934 acres would have been affected each year. Turf-cutting on this scale must have had a great effect on soil nutrition and perpetuated the acid soil community. The loss of soil would also have been instrumental in the creation of the wet areas and pools so important to the dragonflies and other insects.

Open grazing persisted until the Inclosure Acts of 1698 and 1808. This legislation excluded grazing animals from certain areas, thereby allowing the forest regeneration needed by a timber-hungry Navy. This restriction on grazing put enormous pressure on the remaining areas, further limiting any forest regeneration and ensuring the continuation of heathland. By 1851 the Crown relaxed many of the restrictions in the Royal Forest, though the area retained its importance for timber production, a tradition that is perpetuated by the Forestry Commission today.

The forest now supports 2,500 wild deer (fallow, sika, roe and red), 3,500 ponies and 2,000 cattle. It is the relationship between the grazers and the vegetation that produces a very complex ecosystem. This is not a passive relationship, and the effect of large herbivores on an environment can be drastic. The direct consumption of a habitat can destroy it, as is demonstrated by the red deer's destruction of the Scottish wildwood, and there are also more subtle chemical effects exercised in areas where soils lack certain elements. For example, the tiny lemmings of Alaska eat so much of the new plant growth that the soil becomes starved of the elements (nitrogen and phosphorus) it took to produce that growth. Until the death of the animals releases the chemicals back to the soil, plants are poorly nourished and stunted.

Deer have played a similar role in the New Forest. Mature trees in the woodlands can be dated to three periods of reduced grazing: firstly, the time of enclosures to produce ships' timbers; secondly, the period following the Crown's relinquishing of hunting rights, when an attempt was made to eradicate fallow deer from the area; and thirdly between 1930 and 1945 when the Great Depression caused such a drop in stock prices that grazing was greatly reduced.

However, fallow deer populations (by far the most important species) have slumped from 9,000 in 1857 to 2,500 today, while the New Forest ponies have increased. The role of grazing has therefore been shifted towards the New Forest pony. The question is whether the difference in grazing strategies will have adverse effects on the rich and complex ecology of the area. It seems that if anything, the change has been beneficial. Throughout the year the ponies create and maintain the diversity of this habitat.

STREAMSIDE LAWNS

These grassy areas appear artificial, as if prepared by the local authority as picnic areas. They are, in fact, created and maintained by the New Forest ponies. Here, in the short grass, a unique community of prostrate clovers and herbs thrive. Unfortunately this close cropping excludes cattle, and some New Forest cattle owners believe that a review of current grazing practices is needed. The problem of overgrazing has threatened the management system that creates these streamside lawns.

In spring they move to their preferred grazing areas of streamside lawns. At first sight these manicured grasslands beside many streams appear artificial, but this close cropped sward is the work of the versatile pony incisor. These lawns are fertilized and watered during the winter floods, and consequently they are the first areas to produce quality grasses in spring. Years of grazing have caused prostrate herbs and clovers to replace long-stemmed rye grasses. This new habitat has spawned an array of species such as pennyroyal and small fleabane, for which the New Forest is the main distribution centre in Britain today.

During the arid weeks of high summer ponies move to heathland bog where molinia appears relatively succulent. This move is vital as many heathland areas survived agricultural and urban development only to drown under a sea of molinia when traditional management techniques died out. In the New Forest, however, this aggressive grass is kept just below the surface of the heather, allowing a diversity of plants to show. The control of molinia is perhaps the major contribution of the New Forest pony to the heathland ecology.

Winter sees the horses move into gorse break and scrub to gain some protection from the elements. Both gorse and holly are eaten along with the mosses of some deciduous trees. Most horses would find this browse difficult but New Forest ponies have acquired a distinctive technique of browsing gorse without being pricked by their spines. They roll their sensitive top lip out of the way and protrude their incisors as far forward as possible and nip the stem. It seems this behaviour is learnt by foals watching the mares. Browsing in this way produces thick bushes much appreciated by nesting birds. Some species you would expect to find in this scrub are eradicated, such as blackthorn, hawthorn and hazel, while others like holly seem to be more evident than in similar areas that are ungrazed.

Of the other species that could shape the heath, roe deer may significantly suppress new deciduous trees, but red deer are too low in numbers to make much of a contribution. So ponies have successfully assumed the mantle of shapers of the New Forest from the fallow deer. But a problem has been discovered that could have destructive consequences unless it is addressed. It stems from the ponies' penchant for the grassland grazing: 50% of all pony grazing is concentrated on about 5% of the area. The amount taken from this small area often exceeds the growth, resulting in overgrazing. The problem is compounded by the fact that cattle of the forest share the same grasslands, and cattle owners are worried that their stock suffers. Some commoners have called for areas of heath to be ploughed and turned into grassland, but the decline in the economic importance of stock grazing has weakened this argument in the eyes of conservationists. This position reveals the uncertain future of the New Forest. If agricultural interests are assuaged by the creation of new grasslands, then smooth snakes and sand lizards lose vital habitat. If, on the other hand, the economic importance of commoners' grazing is denied, one has to admit that vital land management techniques are a vulnerable relic that might soon disappear. It seems the latter is closer to the truth. Professor Puttman, from the University of Southampton, has shown how the grazing rights within the forest have changed in the last forty years. Until recently two-thirds of the holdings represented the main source of income for the holders. Today only 10% of the holdings are worked full time and 50% of those asked said that less than a tenth of their income came from agriculture. The prized traditional methods of land management of the forest are in danger of becoming no more than an interesting way of life, and one can only hope that a statutory conservation body will take up the reins dropped by the commoners.

What is left of this habitat is precious. The losses in Europe equal those in this country, so its specialist flora and fauna have no other strongholds. Passive protection for heaths is not enough, but at least the New Forest heaths have provided a successful model for future managers to follow.

GOLDEN RINGED DRAGONFLY

This large and spectacular insect hunts mountain and moorland streams by day, and even after dark. Males tour the streams in their territory with a swift and direct flight, hoping to rendezvous with a female. On finding a receptive female the male accompanies her to nearby vegetation for mating. The fertilized eggs are laid in the stream by the female unaided, usually July/August. Once hatched, the large dark-brown nymphs (35–44 mm) hunt for at least two years in the soft substrate, waiting with just their heads exposed for prey items to pass. They emerge on dark nights and will crawl some distance before the adult emerges. Adults are on the wing from June to September.

LARGE RED DAMSELFLY

These insects are on the wing from May to August. Compared to the larger dragonflies their flight is feeble. They rise above the heather for only an instant before taking cover from the breeze. Aggressive males patrol the aquatic marginal vegetation searching for food and mates, attacking all other suitors they find. Once paired, the two insects will remain locked together until the eggs are laid. These hatch soon afterwards, and, like the golden ringed dragonfly, the larvae will hunt the waterway for two years before emerging.

DARTFORD WARBLER

Of all the indicator species for heathland, the Dartford warbler is perhaps the most important, and the future of the species is inextricably linked with the conservation of lowland heaths. Due to the generally low carrying capacities of heathland soils, heaths must be large to present viable ecosystems, and contain mature stands of heather to provide suitable nest sites. Stands of gorse will further enhance heathland, for this plant hosts the density of insects necessary to raise large broods. In this respect the New Forest ponies' manipulation of heathland shrubs towards gorse is of prime importance. The scarcity of this habitat so limits Dartford warblers that the British population is always vulnerable to a severe winter.

STONECHAT

This is another characteristic bird of heathland and scrub, though it is more widespread than the Dartford warbler. In winter, British numbers are swelled by visitors from the Continent and passage migrants. For residents, breeding begins in late March. A cup of grass and moss, lined with wool and feathers, is well concealed at the base of shrubby heathland plants. The five or six eggs are incubated for about two weeks by the female, after which both birds feed the nestling for a further two weeks. In good years a pair may raise three broods, though two is more common.

SILVER STUDDED BLUE

Along with the Dartford warbler and some reptiles, the silver studded blue is a heathland specialist. Habitat loss has destroyed former populations in Kent and mid-Wales, and today its main populations are on the dry heathlands in the south and east, and locally on chalk downs and sandy coasts. Often seen feeding on bell heather, they fly from June to September. Eggs are laid in July on bird's-foot trefoil or gorse. The caterpillars hatch in April and complete five instars before pupating in June. These small stumpy caterpillars produce a sweet secretion that ants find irresistible; in return for this sustenance, the ants provide protection and transport to new foodplants. The butterflies emerge later in June.

SMALL SKIPPER

This small butterfly flies in July and August in rough grassy places. It deposits its eggs inside the sheaths of grasses, where the larvae hibernate until the following spring. After spending the early part of the summer feeding, the caterpillars pupate in June and July. This one is feeding on large bird's-foot trefoil, one of the common flowering plants of the damper grasslands of the New Forest heathlands. This plant carries a cyanide compound to deter grazing, but pollinating insects like the skipper and butterflies of the blue family have developed the required immunity to allow the barter of food for pollination.

COMMON BLUE DAMSELFLY

Mating swarms of this insect may number thousands, and pools throughout the country witness spectacular displays during warm midsummer evenings. During the day males hover over the water, keeping pace with the wind and scanning the area for females. In the evenings common blues may cover the vegetation of the water's margins, and, as the sun dies, they uniformly angle their bodies to catch the last rays so that the bushes sparkle with tens of thousands of iridescent wings. The pairing of these insects allows the male to pull the female from the water after she has inserted the eggs on a plant stem below the water's surface. However, voracious great diving beetles wait to drag exhausted damselflies below. The slim yellow/black or green larvae spend a year under water.

HEDGE BROWN (THE GATEKEEPER)

Though this is meant to be a butterfly of woodlands and hedges, it can commonly be seen on the New Forest heaths. The gatekeeper is not a species that needs protection, nor one that is in great decline, but its beauty is often overlooked when considering its more illustrious cousins. The adults are on the wing from July till the eggs are laid on grasses in August. The species overwinter as larvae, with five instars, and pupate in June.

BOG ASPHODEL

This is a characteristic plant of British bogs and wetlands, anywhere with acid soils. It has been used as a dye for women's hair and as a medicine. The plant was also thought to be the cause of broken bones in sheep, though the lack of calcium in poor heathland soils was actually responsible. Flowering from July to August, bog asphodel can form gorgeous mats of rich colours that stand out from the swards of molinia and heather.

SILVER-Y MOTH

These moths are not easy to see when they are sitting on vegetation, but walking through the heather will flush them out, and then their low fluttering flight is distinctive. They fly by day and night, but are most often seen visiting bell heather at dusk. Silver-Ys do not normally survive a British winter, but immigrants from Europe breed here bolstering the British population in the autumn. The name is derived from the conspicuous white mark resembling a 'Y' on each forewing.

THE DARK BUSH CRICKET

Five species of grasshopper and cricket are found on the New Forest heaths. This particular cricket is the species responsible for much of the chorus that emanates from hedgerows and woodland edge between August and November. The eggs, laid in rotting wood the previous autumn, hatch at the end of April revealing small spider-like creatures. There are five subsequent stages before maturity is reached in July and the calling for mates begins. During its lifecycle the bush cricket eats small spiders and insects as well as plant material. On the wetter parts of the heath, bush crickets co-exist with similar bog crickets, while large marsh grasshoppers inhabit the reedswamps.

EMPEROR MOTH LARVA

This insect is the only British representative of the silk moth family, though the cocoon of the caterpillar is of no commercial value. It is hard to believe how inconspicuous this larva is: its colour blends with young grasses, while the yellow patches break up the outline. The adult female moths fly only at night, while the males fly day and night over the heather that is the insect's foodplant. Both male and female emperor moths are made conspicuous by the large eyespots on all four wings; features said to mimic the eyes of predatory mammals, and so deter birds. The eggs are laid on heather stems, and in May and June the caterpillars emerge to feed until pupation in July and August. In this state emperors overwinter and hatch the following May.

SMOOTH SNAKE

The smooth snake is another lowland heath specialist. Nowhere else in Britain are the winters mild enough to support it, though it is widespread on the Continent. Most species of reptile need to bask to raise and maintain their body temperature, but the smooth snake's thin body precludes the need to bask in direct sunlight, making it difficult to find. This, and the colour variations in the grass snake, prevented its discovery in Britain until 1853. By 1868 it was thought locally common, but loss of habitat has made the contemporary British population of this snake very vulnerable. It is active by day, hunting small lizards and young snakes of other species. Smooth snakes pair in spring and August sees them give birth to between two and fifteen young, of five to six inches in length. Its name is derived from the lack of ridges or keels that are present in the scales of most snakes.

SAND LIZARD

On the Continent the sand lizard can live at altitudes of up to 2,000 feet, but Britain's cool damp summers limit it to the low-lying coastal dunes and sandy heaths that give it its name. On the New Forest heaths its preference for hunting in taller stands of heather make it difficult to find. The best time to see sand lizards is early morning when they bask on pathways and open sun spots. They do, however, avoid the midday sun and may stop basking during the hottest days of summer. Underneath the heather they inhabit tunnels, self-dug or abandoned by rodents. Here, in July, an average of eight eggs (with shells like parchment) are buried and left to incubate. By August they are hatched. People are often surprised by the size of sand lizards; they are at least one third longer than the common lizard. This, and the vibrant green of the male in its mating garb, makes identification easy.

WAVY HAIR GRASS

This slender and graceful
perennial favours the peaty
soils of heath and moorland.
On the small heathlands in
the Mendips it grows in
profusion. Here, in July, the
tip of the slender stem
branches into many wavy,
cotton-thin branches. Each
one of these carries seeds,
and, as they catch the late rays
of evening sunlight, specks of
light seem to dance as the
plants sway with the breeze.

HEATHER AND BRACKEN

On the higher parts of the heath, bracken and heather dominate sandy soils. On summer walks through these low hills the air is full of the calls of insects, and the dust from the parched earth. The bracken seen here was once used as bedding for stock, but now it spreads over the hills unchecked. Heather communities, rich in wildlife, are gradually overpowered by the relatively poor bracken communities. This is of concern to many conservationists, but large-scale eradication of this persistent plant is very expensive.

SUNDEWS

These carnivorous plants supplement the food gleaned from the peaty soils by digesting insects. The red droplets on each leaf are mistaken by midges as water where they can lay their eggs, but once contact is made they are enmeshed in a sticky trap until the leaf folds around their exhausted body. Juices secreted by the leaf then digest the body and the husk is discarded a couple of days later. It is estimated that each sundew can take as many as 2,000 flies in a summer. These plants can be found in bogs all over the country, but seem particularly prolific on these southern heath bogs. This is probably due to the density of prey species that this mild climate permits. The sundew is a good indicator of the health of bog: in areas where conifer afforestation or agriculture has proved detrimental to mire ecosystems, a fall in the density of sundews has proved an early warning sign.

FARMLAND NEAR MARLBOROUGH DOWNS

Farmland abandoned by Neolithic man has been returned to production by modern methods of agriculture. The discovery of fertilizers returned exhausted soil to economic profitability, and so displaced creatures like smooth snakes and sand lizards. Today, Britain retains a mere quarter of the heathland that was present 200 years ago.

• ESTUARY •

THE RIVER BRUE

The confluence of the Rivers Brue and Parret create mud flats much used by wading birds. The straightening of the River Brue and the erection of lock gates was possibly England's first nationally funded capital project. Though this attempt to stop the flooding of the Levels' farmland proved unsuccessful, it was the beginning of a process that would ultimately drain the Levels. The turbidity of these waters makes them unsuitable for commercial activity, and the difficulty for shipping is highlighted by the Brue. This river once had a port in the town of Highbridge, where lumber was landed for the local saw mill, Woodbry and Hains. But as the factory turned to road transport, the silt carried by this river system changed the port from an excellent elver fishing venue into grassy pastures of sheep's fescue in fifteen years.

GLOBALLY, ESTUARIES SHOW such variation that it is hard to stretch one definition over them all. From the giants like the Amazon, responsible for 20% of all freshwater discharged into the sea, to more humble British examples, they are all products of their own special circumstances. There are three main causes of estuaries: the sea's invasion of subsiding land, as in the drowned tectonic plateline of San Francisco Bay; the creation of a shallow brackish sea when the outflow of several rivers is obscured by a sand bar, as in the Waddenzee of north-west Europe; and the drowning of river valleys by the post-glacial rise in sea level. This last feature is behind most British estuaries, but each example is further modified by local features. For instance, while the drowned valleys of southern England produce the wide gentle estuaries of the Severn or Southampton Water, further north the same invasion of glacial valleys produces sheer-sided Scottish lochs. This allied with variations in local geology make every estuary unique.

Britain's 150 estuaries are unrivalled anywhere in Europe for their diversity of form. Such diversity coupled with the mild winters afforded by the Gulf Stream create the perfect wintering grounds for 18 million birds. Some resident birds move here for winter feeding; others are winter visitors escaping harsh conditions further north and east; and many use the estuaries as feeding stations on the great spring and autumn migrations between the breeding grounds of Scandinavia, Iceland, Siberia and Greenland and wintering grounds in Africa and southern Europe. Incredibly, these huge population movements are fuelled by the strip of land between high and low tide. This area of mud flat and salt marsh is one of the most productive habitats on earth producing food for wildfowl and waders in massive amounts. A flock of 5,000 shelduck will eat 15 million small shellfish (hydrobia) in one low-tide period. If you scale 5,000 up to 18 million, you reach the output figure for just one day.

This output is achieved despite one of the most severe environments in Britain. Organisms have to cope with a part-aquatic, part-terrestrial environment, where the salinity rockets twice a day. Habitats may be submerged in silt, scoured by strong currents, baked in a summer sun, intensified by a film of water or chilled by winter winds.

These are also complex systems with ever-changing conditions. Salinity gradients vary not only from estuary mouth upstream, but also from high- to low-water mark, and from summer to winter. Not even the water is homogenous. The lower levels carry so much silt that they are little more than sluggish troughs of liquid mud, while clearer, faster water runs above carrying more salt, oxygen and photosynthesizing organisms.

Animals that actually live in the salt marsh and mud flats (birds and some fish only visit) show a number of adaptations to this constantly changing environment. The hard shells of crustaceans present an effective barrier to the fluctuating salinity, while molluscs, like the hydrobia, vary the internal level of amino acids in an effort to stabilize the osmotic pressures. The common activity of burrowing helps to create a more stable micro climate and protects against wave action, but breeding often takes place in the more stable deep sea. One Chinese crab travels 700 miles to breed, a journey which takes the males three months (the females die in deep water after spawning). Though this is an extreme example, many British crabs make shorter journeys to still water, while many British fish find the abundant food and protected environment a perfect nursery.

The creation of this salt marsh/mud flat habitat depends on conditions exemplified by river estuaries. Their partially internal location protects these soft structures from wave action and weather; while the river and tides provide the building material, silt. The type of estuary produced depends on which water system is dominant. Muddy estuaries develop where the river flow prevails over the tide; sand and shingle banks are tidal structures. Of the two, the river-dominated estuary is the most productive and it is on this type that we will concentrate.

The slow flow of a mature river keeps only the smallest particles in suspension. These particles are finally laid to rest by a mixture of physics and chemistry. When sea and freshwater meet, an electrochemical binding pulls together sediments into clumps that fall to the bottom. A moving tide keeps this material liquid, but the still water of high tide sees silt settle to a consistency of clotted cream. Mud flats deposited in this intertidal zone escape the worst scouring effect of low water. If they escape storms or changes in current, pioneering plants such as glasswort, eel grass and spartina stabilize the beds. This is the first phase in a transition from mud flats to salt marsh. As wind is slowed by a forest, the foliage of these plants slows the water flow, causing faster deposition. As each tide leaves its subsequent layer the marsh begins to rise, reducing the amount of time salt water covers it. Eventually the 'land' rises above the level of a normal high tide. Throughout this process the plant communities keep pace with species less tolerant of salt and daily inundation, replacing their forebears. The gradual change in the plant communities from low-to high-water mark reflects this chronological change. Beginning on the low flats eel grass, glasswort and spartina communities give way to spartina, thrift and sea aster communities. Further up, common salt marsh and other grazed grasses give way to the top plant community of herb-rich meadows. These areas escape all but the storm tides and therefore host plants with the lowest saline tolerance. These plant communities include sea milkwort, sea rush and bulbous foxtail grass. If left long enough, the saline plant communities may be replaced by the terrestrial vegetation for that environment, often heathland or grassland. In this way the salt marsh appears to grow towards the estuary centre, with heathland turning to woodland on the landside and mudflat becoming salt marsh on the seaward side. Either this process continues until the river finds a new route, as with the Mississippi delta, or an equilibrium is reached between erosion and deposition.

Whatever the salt marsh's long-term geological fate, its ecological nature is fuelled by the plant communities. Dying salt marsh grasses feed algae, phytoplankton and microbes. This soup feeds bacteria, which in turn feed the filter-feeders: ciliata, shellfish, and omnivores like crabs. At the top of the food chain are the predators, birds and fish.

The striking thing about the system is the sheer amount of food produced. The impoverished systems of lowland heaths or upland moors rely upon consumers replacing the nutrients they eat. British estuaries see 18 million birds taking energy out of the system and yet their predation has little effect on the numbers of gastropods. This richness relies upon the twice daily sluicing of organic matter by the sea and the river, ensuring plenty at the base of the food chain.

The ubiquity of this food source, for a long time a great strength, has in recent years become its weakness. The seeds of this change were sown with the development of coastal settlements in Britain. The protection that makes salt marsh practicable also attracts industry and people, and the waste products of both. Originally Britain's colonists settled at river heads. For hundreds of years these settlements thrived as traditional trading posts and river crossing points, but over the last hundred years populations have shifted downstream. The growth of international trade, bulk shipping, and the rising costs of transporting raw materials has made deep-water harbours a necessity for many industries. The scale of the recent industrial complexes has also had an effect. Oil refineries, nuclear power stations and the like have become too thirsty for upstream locations. Add to this an estuary's protection from the rigours of the weather and its apparent ability to 'flush' large amounts of untreated effluent and the economics become irresistible. Of course, these industries attracted a workforce that produced their own waste and this allied to industry makes pollution an unfortunate characteristic of the modern urban estuary. Initially the system appears to withstand pollution quite well. It seems the ability of marine organisms lower down the food chain to withstand brackish water has given them some resistance to pollution. However, far from being an

PUFFINS

These birds spend most of their year out at sea, but March finds them gathering in great rafts off shore. Here, already sporting brightly coloured breeding bills, they pair prior to coming ashore and digging the egg-laying chamber (they may use a rabbit burrow). The single egg is laid in April and after forty-three days' incubation and fifty days in the nest the birds head out to sea. Lundy Island is the last stronghold for auks in the Bristol Channel, though even here numbers are in decline. Even the massive colony on Skokholm Island (20,000 in 1931) has shown drastic reductions. The reasons for these declines are not known, but oil spills and diminishing food supplies must have had some effect.

advantage, this merely allows them to carry small doses of poison to predators further up the food chain. The vast numbers of prey items consumed by predators can concentrate these poisons and may result in abnormalities or death. This process was tragically illustrated by the inhabitants of Minimata Bay in Japan, which received crippling and fatal doses of mercury from local shellfish.

Apart from toxicity, pollutants such as crude oil may smother animals. Though the most harrowing examples of this are flashed across our television screens with each oil spill, more insidious examples take place in all our estuaries. The Severn Estuary, for example, suffered regular spills of fuel oil throughout the seventies, killing 10% of the overwintering scooters, while salt marsh plants of Southampton Water have died as a result of repeated coatings from local refineries. Because of the reduction in wave action, estuaries are not oxygen-rich environments, making de-oxygenation one of the most insidious forms of pollution. It has been shown that the sewage discharge into the River Tees reduces the oxygen by 71,000 pounds a day, or to put it more graphically the amount of oxygen needed by 893,461,000 cubic feet of sea water.

There are a whole host of other pressures inflicted by the modern industrial complex. Large boats have brought alien stowaways that invade our estuaries, often aided by the discharge of warm water used in cooling processes. Southampton Water is said to host more foreign bodies than native. The ever-increasing size of vessels has also led to dredging of these silty areas, which upsets the established system of deposition and erosion.

The Severn Estuary

The River Severn begins its life on the sphagnum beds of the hills above Plynlimon, in the Cambrian Mountains, and reaches the sea in one of Britain's largest estuaries; one that it shares with the Rivers Usk, Wye, Parret and Avon. The estuary's funnel shape gathers the unimpeded surge of 3,700 miles of the Atlantic, creating one of the largest tidal ranges in the world. This, allied to the gentle slopes of the estuary, produces a huge inter-tidal zone exposing miles of mud flat and salt marsh to hungry birds. Today's estuary is the flood plain of a younger, more vigorous river that cut a deepwater channel (now used by shipping) when fuelled by glacial meltwater. The seas rose, drowning not only the flood plain but 200 square miles of Somerset, forming the Somerset levels and moors.

The river is the main source of sediment for the Severn's expansive mud flats, but due to the strong currents of the system the 10 million tonnes of silt it carries are continually redistributed. With each slack tide some liquid mud solidifies, and not all of it is reactivated with the new tide. In some cases, mud banks grow and become colonized, but often new mud flats are broken up by the tides. As it is, the sediment/tidal forces in the Severn estuary are in equilibrium and the flats produce food for the millions of birds that regularly winter here. Ten square feet of Bridgewater Bay will contain more than 10 million nematode worms, as well as other important prey items such as lugworm, ragworm, Baltic tellin and the hydrobia so important for the 2,000 shelduck that winter on the estuary. Different waders possess different length bills and so exploit species at differing depths. The long-billed curlew reaches deepest for lug and rag worms, while the shorter billed species like knots consume shallow burrowing shellfish such as Baltic tellin.

The Welsh coast of the Bristol Channel boasts impressive numbers of birds using the mixture of sand and mud flat: 8,600 waders on the Milford Haven complex and 20,000 in Carmarthen Bay. The sandy areas of the Burry Inlett produce cockle populations supporting 38,000 waders in total, including an internationally significant number of oystercatchers (15,000) and pintail (650). The sand flats of Swansea Bay and the mud flats of the Taw and Torrige are home to dunlin and ringed plover.

In the Severn Estuary strong tides scour most prey species from the sand and rocks, making the sheltered deposition areas of the Welsh Grounds and Bridgewater Bay the most important feeding places for waders. The peak population is 88,500 birds with nine species occurring in internationally important numbers. Of the marine birds the most significant population is the 25,000 common scooters that overwinter and moult in Carmarthen Bay. As has already been mentioned, these have been seriously reduced in recent years. In fact pollution is the cause of a serious decline in many marine populations (along with a suspected decline in the productivity of traditional feeding grounds). The island of Lundy once hosted an important population of sea birds. In 1939 there were: 19,000 pairs of guillemots; 10,500 pairs of razorbills; and 3,500 pairs of puffins. Today Lundy retains only 1,000 pairs of guillemots and 300 pairs of puffins. Oil is the likely culprit, accounting for 5,000 auks between 1974 and 1980. Shags and kittiwakes now breed on the old auk breeding sites. While the smothering qualities of oil have hit truly marine species, it is the toxic effects of pollution that are the future threat to estuarine birds. The most toxic substance found in the food chain for birds (we have long since stopped eating the shellfish of Clevedon owing to the bacteriological pollution from sewage) was cadmium, probably because it persists in the gut, but all manner of effluent finds its way into the estuary. Lead, chromium, copper, mercury, nickle, zinc and PCBs all rely on the flush capabilities of the estuary to carry them out to sea, but this may change if present proposals are carried out.

In recent years the awareness of how 'dirty' traditional energy production was, along

GANNETS

The gannet preys on surface-feeding fish, dropping from considerable heights with spectacular dives. In the turbid waters of the Severn Estuary this would never be possible. However, the gannet's ability to make long feeding trips permitted a sizeable colony on Lundy Island. A decline in the colony was first noticed in 1871, and despite efforts to save it, nesting ceased in 1909. There are two explanations: firstly, better conditions on the new colony on Grassholm Island off the Welsh coast, plus the limited interference from man on the new island lured birds away from the Bristol Channel; secondly the decline in birds on the western side of the Atlantic reduced British numbers. The 'cropping' of gannet chicks was a traditional activity on both sides of the Atlantic, and the Birds Rock colony in Gulf of St Lawrence, Canada, was reduced from 110,000 pairs in 1834 to 860 in 1889.

SHAGS

Shags and kittiwakes seem to have moved into the old auk nesting sites on Lundy and in 1973 ninety pairs of shag and 1,400 pairs of kittiwakes nested here. This might have something to do with the better adaptations these birds have for feeding in turbid waters, though a general rise in shag numbers all over Britain has probably been caused by a cessation in persecution. From March onwards, nests that seem a critique of man's disregard for his environment cover favoured rocky cliffs; anything is piled on – the plastic that links together cans of beer appears to be a favourite item. As with all cormorants there is no brood patch, so the three or four eggs are incubated with the heat from the large webbed feet. In thirty days the eggs hatch and are tended by both parents for the next fifty-five days until the fledgelings leave the nest.

with a fear of nuclear power, has made alternative sources very attractive. The most common scheme proposed for the Severn is a tidal barrage from Brean-Down to South Lavernock Point. The incoming tide would be allowed through large sluice gates, and then the regulated egress would be used to drive generators. Various committees have looked into the scheme (the most recent commissioned by the construction consortium, the Department of Energy and the Central Electricity Generating Board and the consensus seems to be that a barrage is feasible) though the economic value of the scheme is uncertain and the effect on the local community and the environment must still be ascertained. The current environmental predictions are that a barrage would reduce turbidity thereby increasing the rate of deposition on both sides of the barrage. The reduced rate of flow would obviously reduce flush capabilities and conservative estimates for the increase in pollutants show cadmium up by 56%, nickel by 65% and copper may reach very serious levels. Many heavy metals are deposited by atmospheric pollution, making a reduction at source very difficult. There is also the worry that toxins presently locked in mud flats will be released when deposition patterns are disturbed.

The obstruction to the incoming tide would also drastically reduce the tidal surge, and along with it the massive intertidal mud flats so important to birds. Doctor Ferns of the Department of Zoology at University College, Cardiff, carrying out his own study on the effects of a barrage, reports that 60% of the upstream flats would be lost, though this may be partially ameliorated by an increase in the productivity of those that remain. The consensus picture describes an increase in salt marsh at the expense of mud flat with reed beds dominating the upper reaches of the marsh. The diminished water flow on the marine side of the barrage would cover the scoured rocks of the central channels with layers of silt and affect salinity for 18 miles out to sea. In the light of these far-reaching consequences, the question of whether we need a new source of power becomes pertinent, especially as average consumption could be drastically reduced by more efficient use of energy.

Such problems are not unique to estuaries; the pressures of industrial development and pollution exist throughout Great Britain. But the protection of estuaries presents some special problems. An estuary's population is not indigenous, and so its connection to the country may appear tenuous. In these circumstances it is often difficult to convince the uncommitted that sacrifices are worthwhile. However, if we can, then conservation has taken a great step forward, for to appreciate the special features of the Severn takes an international understanding that follows species across national boundaries. On account of this, conservation of these large estuaries and the bolstering of international conservation law may go hand in hand.

OYSTERCATCHER

These birds are common throughout the Severn Estuary, but reach their highest densities on the Bury inlet, north of Worm's Head. Here, stable sands support their favoured prey of suspension-feeding invertebrates (cockles), and the oystercatcher population reaches 15,000. Some 10,000 oystercatches were shot between 1972 and 1974 in an effort to protect the local cockle industry, but it had little effect on bird numbers. Ironically the number of birds increased with the number of cockles, indicating that both species fluctuate in tune to an outside variable and not each other.

THE MUD FLATS OF SEVERN BEACH

The gentle slopes of the Severn Estuary are the flood plain of an old glacial river. The shallow gradient and strong tides create an immense tidal range. For a 32-foot rise in depth the tide might cover 2,600 feet in distance. This range creates one of the biggest feeding areas for estuarine birds in the British Isles. The quantity of food provided by these areas is astounding, with thousands of prey items per square metre. However, if the Severn barrage is ever built, these areas may disappear.

BLACK-BACKED GULL CHICKS

Black-backed gulls are voracious predators, taking puffins, shearwaters and young rabbits, as well as considerable amounts of human refuse. They nest on sea cliffs, where two to three eggs are laid in May/June. The chicks hatch after twenty-seven days' incubation and are tended by the adults for a further seven weeks. Excluding Dyfed and West Glamorgan, about 200,000 gulls winter in and around the Bristol Channel, and 42,160 gulls breed there. The largest colonies are on Steep Holm, Flat Holm and Steart Islands. In 1980 serious declines in gull populations were recorded (herring gulls by 67%, black-backed gulls by 30%). Botulism is suspected to have been the cause. As yet the source is unknown, though there have been studies showing how the black bin liner has acted as a breeding ground for the organism.

SEA ASTER

This salt marsh plant was widely favoured for garden cultivation in Elizabethan times, but it was usurped by the michaelmas daisy from North America. A plant of mature salt marsh which needs protection from general tidal buffeting, it is best seen towards the end of September. General grazing on the upper saltings has reduced the bluish carpet that once covered the upper salt marsh, but where animals are excluded (for example, at Cardiff Docks) the display can be spectacular. In folk medicine the roots were used to cure wounds.

Bee Orchid

On the dunes of Burnham-on-Sea and Berrow, the stabilization of dunes has reached the stage where scrub communities of marram grass and sea buckthorn have created the calcareous soils favoured by the bee orchid. The flower of this plant resembles a female bumble bee and therefore tempts males to mate. While doing so, pollen is attached to the insects, ensuring the plant's propagation. British bee orchids, however, nearly always pollinate themselves before bees are needed. These perennials flower in June and July.

COLONIZING PINES

Sea buckthorn is not the only plant capable of stabilizing dunes. At Freshfields on Merseyside the National Trust manage a pine plantation that has anchored these dunes for over a hundred years. These woodlands now support a thriving population of red squirrels. Had a different plant been chosen, then a different ecological community would have moved in. In Hampshire, dunes were stabilized by heather creating the lowland heath favoured by sand lizards and smooth snakes, while in Somerset the invasion of dune slacks by reeds formed excellent reedswamp for reed and sedge warblers.

REDSHANK AND DUNLIN

High tide on the Clevedon foreshore sees dunlin and redshank roosting together. The redshank is present in Britain as a resident, a winter visitor and a passage migrant. Birds from Iceland winter here, but also use our estuaries as fuelling stops on journeys to wintering grounds in the Mediterranean and North Africa. Birds from the Continent often shelter here during the more severe weather. There are subtle differences in plumage between the species, with British birds showing less contrast in plumage than redshank from overseas. Most of the large flocks of dunlin seen on British estuaries are almost certainly birds that have left their breeding grounds in the Arctic, northern Scandinavia and Siberia to winter here. A staggering 64,250 dunlin (a significant portion of the world's population) have been recorded in the Severn Estuary and Bristol Channel.

REED BEDS

The reed is a rhizome plant and 50% of its biomass is buried. Where the rhizomes become established, reed stands can spread over extensive areas. On the estuary today, stands of phragmite communities are fairly common on the upper reaches of the River Severn, and high on some salt marshes. Reedswamp is an important habitat for birds such as the reed warbler, but in marine locations reeds are most significant for their ability to trap silt, and so stabilize salt marsh. The plume of seeds appears in August and the seeds are ripe by October. In the past, the use of reed thatching, fencing and even furniture-making has made it one of the few estuarine plants with commercial potential. This habitat will increase dramatically if the Severn barrage is built.

SAND DUNES

Sands blown inshore form a series of hills that become more permanent as you progress inland. Closest to the sea are the embryo dunes; these are features of the strand (the area between high and storm tides). At this stage, any obstruction to the wind will gather sand particles on the leeward side. Plants such as couch grass then colonize, and the dune grows till the next storm moves it further inland. At this second stage, the dunes are semi-permanent, stabilized by marram grass. Plants of this system must be tolerant of a low water table and inorganic soil. Their strategies include germinating in autumn and flowering in spring to avoid the arid summer months, having large root systems, an ability to grow quickly if buried by moving sand, and very efficient nitrogen fixation to overcome the organic deficiencies in the soil. Eventually, dunes support scrub vegetation and this process has produced some valuable heaths.

GLASSWORT (MARSH SAMPHIRE)

In the Bristol Channel this plant marks the development of salt marsh. The glasswort is the first plant to colonize the shifting silt. As the muds stabilize, plants that were once pioneers become engulfed by land as these have. The glasswort was once used in glass-making as a source of bicarbonate of soda, in a process probably imported from Europe. In the sixteenth century ashes of the plant were fused with sand to make a very poor-quality glass. The plant can be eaten boiled or pickled in vinegar. Boatmen on the River Brue used the leaves and stems to brew a tea that they insisted kept off the flu, though what it did for your stomach they never said.

SHELDUCK

Some 3,500 shelduck use the Severn Estuary to winter, to breed and as a safe area to moult. (These moulting birds are on their way to Heligoland Bight in West Germany.) They sift the surface silt in search of small shellfish, hydrobia. At high tide, when the feeding grounds are covered, they congregate on the sandbanks or form rafts that gently drift with the tide. This photograph was taken in Bridgewater Bay, where the Parret meets the Severn. Apart from feeding areas, the estuary provides safe nest sites at Flat Holm and Steep Holm. Around May eight to fifteen eggs are laid in an old rabbit burrow or similar site. Incubation is twenty-eight to thirty days, after which the young are led to water. At sea they aggregate into large groups with only one or two adults remaining.

HINKLEY POINT

The supplies of water and shelter from rough seas have attracted four power stations to the Severn Estuary, one at Berkley, one at Oldbury and two at Hinkley Point. The microclimate created by warm water emissions from these installations has a number of environmental effects: firstly, it precludes those species that find the Severn's natural temperature barely cool enough (for example, the dog whelk); secondly, it maintains alien species from warmer waters; and thirdly, it causes the phenomenon of giantism, evidenced by prawns that grow huge on the unnaturally enriched plankton. However, greater concern should be devoted to the 1,000,000 fish, 5,000,000 prawns and 10 tonnes of shrimps crushed against the inlet screens each year.

• WETLAND •

SOUTHLAKE MOOR

Here, the moor is swathed in the mist of high summer. Under that mist, lapwing, redshank, snipe, curlew and less common waders are raising their broods. The soft muds and high water table allow the chicks to feed easily, and the area's predominantly dairy use limits the amount of fertilizer used.

INCREASE THE WATER content of a habitat and a whole new community of plants and animals, modified to exploit the new opportunities, will move in. Whether the land is merely wet underfoot (marsh), permanently submerged (swamp), or dominated by peaty soil (fen and bog), each will host its own specialities. But these distinctions are to some extent artificial, with a variety of wetland types co-existing in many areas. However, in an attempt to define the area of scrutiny for this chapter I will outline some definitions.

The world's wetlands fall into two broad categories: those that fringe large bodies of water, such as the reedswamps around lakes and rivers, or the salt marshes of oceans; and wetlands that may exist some distance from water, often referred to as 'terrestrial wetlands'. The aquatic marginal habitats of the first category have already been discussed in the previous chapter, leaving us to concentrate on terrestrial wetlands here.

Though all terrestrial wetlands are maintained by intermittent flooding, they may be sub-divided into peatlands (see pp. 45–69) and marshland. The latter occur in warm climes where poor drainage and/or seasonal flooding keep the lower strata of the soil waterlogged, but where seasonal drought allows the higher strata to dry out. During this dry period, bacteria break down the surface layers preventing the accumulation of peat. The nutrients released from the decaying plants, plus deposition from rich floodwaters, create good surface soils with a much wider variety of plants than is found on peat wetlands. Below the surface, however, soils show more evidence of waterlogging. Here the pores are often filled with water, preventing plant decay through oxidation. In this situation microbes use nitrates, sulphate and carbon dioxide in place of oxygen. These anaerobic soils are easy to spot as the reddish pigmentation of iron oxide is missing, leaving the grey-blue soils characteristic of river banks and estuaries. Further evidence of this substitution is the stench of rotten eggs emanating from the black sludge at the bottom of ditches and ponds. Here sulphides have replaced oxygen, producing black iron sulphide soils with the accompanying hydrogen sulphide smell.

Plants in these regions encounter two problems. While difficulties of intermittent (usually winter) submersion are obviated through overwintering as seeds, many plants are still obliged to root at lower levels where the low oxygen content requires some modification. Some plants carry oxygen down from the upper structures to their roots, and plants such as willow herb can grow auxiliary roots near the water's surface during summer floods increasing oxygen uptake. This transference is evidenced by the hard casing found around plant roots in marshy areas. The casing is built up by precipitations of iron, and other chemicals oxidizing on contact with oxygen 'leaking' from these roots. Apart from the lack of oxygen the anaerobic metabolisms of soil bacteria produce toxic by-products, resulting in toxin-resistant plants. For example, cross-leaved heath replaces ordinary heather on wet moorland because heather cannot tolerate the build up of un-oxidized iron that is the result of wet conditions.

Semi-aquatic plants must attack the problem at a more fundamental level and change their metabolisms in favour of non-oxygen chemistry. Water lilies, for example, are faced with the problem of rooting in anaerobic soils, and obtain their oxygen above the water's surface. However, at the start of each growing season they exist only as roots and must fuel the growth to the surface and supplies of oxygen. This is achieved by fermenting carbohydrate and accepting the toxic by-products until the surface is reached.

As with most ecologies the wetland community of animals and plants rests upon unspectacular, but none the less important organisms. Soil invertebrates, though not interesting in themselves, carry out vital tasks in the ecosystem, aerating soil and making nutrients available to plants. Most of this work is completed by air-breathing organisms that must cope with reduced oxygen. The necessary modifications include trapping a thin layer of air around the body (springtails); tapping plant roots (mosquito larvae); or the increase in efficiency of haemoglobin as propounded by some small worms. Most of these communities will fluctuate in depth with the height of the water table.

If the modifications of the soil invertebrates and plants succeed, then a canopy community can develop. Though not many of us will see rarities like swallowtail butterflies, the metallic gaudiness and characteristic rustle of the dragonflies and damselflies on hot summer days, or the singing of crickets at night are sights and sounds for all. However, many of the creatures up in this canopy are not unique to wetland, but infiltrate from the surrounding countryside. Shrews and voles are attracted by the abundant insect life and lush vegetation, but each has its more aquatically adapted cousin the water vole and shrew. Of course there are the frogs and toads that must return to breed, and these bring with them the grass snake that is just as at home on dry heaths. If you are lucky, you may catch a glimpse of an otter or mink, but generally the soft substrate excludes large predators. Perhaps because of this, wetlands have become havens for many species of birds. The soft soil, rich in invertebrates, attracts many of the same species described in the Estuary chapter. The soft soil becomes the training ground for chicks that must find their food in the top half an inch or die, and, of course, if the water table falls, the surface invertebrates fall with it.

Though a drop in the water table has been the most common threat to wetlands, there are others. Water quality is as important as quantity. This is a difficult area for conservation as the catchment area for a modest river may be thousands of square miles, and a wetland may be fed by several rivers. The Norfolk Broads, home of the swallowtail butterfly, has been badly damaged by Norwich's pollution of the River Yare.

Historically one of the problems for marshland has been that its fertile soils have been coveted by farmers. Though this may have been of ecological benefit in a few cases, such as the Hampshire water meadows, it is no accident that agriculture's first steps in England were taken in the fenlands of East Anglia and the Somerset Levels.

THE SOMERSET LEVELS

If you were to draw a line around Taunton, Weston Super Mare, Glastonbury and South Petherton it would enclose the Somerset Levels and moors. The coastal 'levels' are just above sea level; further inland the moors sink well below the high tide mark of Bridgewater Bay. In this land of straight roads and sodden fields, seven sluggish rivers try to discharge into the Bristol Channel. In winter, water-laden clouds from the Atlantic burst over the landscape and the Rivers Axe, Brue, Carey, Isle, Tone, Parrett and Yeo breach their banks. From October to March, drainage ditches and rivers seep onto the fields and 150,000 acres from Taunton to the Mendips become the 'last great English fen'. This landscape is a delicate balance between man and water that has lasted over a thousand years.

Monks arrived at Muchelney in the fourth century, seeking a life of contemplation in a land of mist and water. By the Conquest, seven centuries had seen a growth in the local population. These people valued the rich summer pastures and grew impatient with winter flooding. At this time fisheries were common and those of Creech St Michael and North Curry dammed the floodwater allowing drainage only through netted channels. This irked dairymen eager to graze their herds and the conflict between water and agriculture began. In the course of time the fisheries were ousted and the great fen began to shrink.

For a long time the land resisted. Most landowners were content to bolster river banks, protecting their own land. It was not until the eighteenth century, when the people of Highbridge built lock gates on the River Brue, that the fen's whole nature was finally threatened. As a method of reducing river levels the lock failed, but it marked the beginning of large centrally funded schemes that would eventually succeed.

Today pumps and irrigation channels have drained most of the landscape, but enough

SOUTHLAKE MOOR IN FLOOD

The drainage and embankment of the River Parret were well under way by 1234, though to this day controlled flooding still occurs. Winter rains have swollen the River Parret, and to protect farmland elsewhere sluices are opened and Southlake Moor is submerged. This keeps the ground soft for wader chicks in the summer and provides wintering areas for birds.

water escapes to keep bits of the wetland ecology alive. And what an ecology it is. For birds it is a place to overwinter and to breed. You can still see water rail and nightjar; and lapwing, redshank and curlew all breed on the sunken peatlands. Some unimproved damp meadows continue to provide a haven for orchids, and drainage channels provide a reservoir for wetland and bog plants. It is still my Christmas tradition to walk the levees of the River Parret. In December the surrounding moors are flooded. A huge lake spreads beneath the slate-grey skies and only incongruous lines of bare trees and five-bar gates mark the drowned fields. Watching skeins of Bewick's swans and teal, the scene is timeless. On days like these, looking south to Burrow Mump, the mythical tales of pagan Somerset and King Arthur seem almost credible.

Though much of the area is true marshland, sphagnum mosses once grew in some hollows of the Brue basin, creating small peat bogs. While the marshland is threatened by drainage, these bogs are at the mercy of peat cutters. My memories of peat cutting are of a quaint operation, but today machines tear out peat at the rate of 80 tonnes per day. As a result 60% of the plant extinction on the Levels has occurred on low-lying peat moors. Some of the remaining areas have been given protection, but, as with so many delicate habitats, if the protected area is too small then action outside the reserve can have disastrous consequences. The problem is that peatland ecology relies on this soil's ability to hold water at an unnaturally high level, like a sponge in a saucer of water. Extracting peat obviously leaves holes which fill with water, and to continue digging, these workings must be pumped dry day and night. When digging is close to a reserve, water loss from that reserve leaves it literally high and dry. As water flows out, the peat dries and cracks, the plants die and the soil is blown on the wind. If the destruction continues we will lose bog pimpernel, sundew, butterwort, lesser butterfly orchid, heath spotted orchid, devil's bit and their respective insect life. Street Heath, Shapwick Heath, Catcott and Westhay – not one of these important peatland sites is unaffected. Today the last remnant of active raised bog in Somerset occurs on the east side of Shapwick Heath and peat is cut on its borders to the north and west.

Wetlands are such vulnerable habitats that they just cannot survive this treatment. A 2-inch fall in the water table could kill myriad species of plant and invertebrate life, and each change is magnified in the food chain. The rapid deterioration of the Levels has stretched this chain to breaking point. Since 1890 more than 100 plant species have suffered, and many are now extinct.

In an effort to halt the decline, two types of legislation have been introduced. These create sites of special scientific interest (SSSI) and environmentally sensitive areas (ESA). Within ESAs, grants are awarded to farmers who avoid pesticides and produce a hay crop. The move from traditional haymaking to silage production has resulted in much earlier cutting, destroying wild flowers before they have a chance to seed. This has reduced meadows to drab monocultures of rye grass. While the late cutting allows time for wild plants to mature, insecticide-free fields provide homes for insects needed for pollination. Unfortunately, as measures taken to ensure the maintenance of high water tables, the SSSIs have failed. The first thing to understand is that the system of control that spreads over this part of the country has the complications of evolution, not the simplicity of design. It must be remembered that since the sixth century farmers and local people have toiled against winter flooding, desperate to improve the agricultural economy. Pitted against this tradition, conservation was always likely to find life uncomfortable. While conservation bodies were trying to raise water levels, other statutory bodies, charged with increasing agricultural output, were giving capital grants for projects that lowered it. In the final analysis, the British legal system gave great powers to the landowner and so the interests of the farmers prevailed. Water levels fell drastically throughout the 1960s and 70s. The predictable consequence is a ground too hard for the chicks of ground-nesting waders to feed. In fact, their prey items have been forced beyond the range of their bills. To give you an example of the fall in numbers, the early Seventies saw forty pairs of snipe breed on the Tealham and Tadham moor; in 1991 there were eleven and of those only one pair was successful. Even the more common birds have suffered. Fields that hosted breeding redshank in 1983 were stony, hard and silent in 1990.

The advent of the National Rivers Authority has improved matters and water levels are being maintained. But this fragile ecology needs balance and since the 1970s the balance of the past 1,000 years has been badly upset. With recent moves away from intensive farming I hope that water levels will be allowed to rise still further, for 'the last great English fen' cannot afford to shrink further.

POLLARDED WILLOWS

Probably the most evocative sight of the Levels – pollarded willows over water. Periodically (every five to seven years), the branches of the crown are cut back to the trunk. Failure to do so results in the trunk splitting from the excessive weight. This practice does, however, have its dangers: if it is carried out too late, then it might disturb nesting birds; and the use of mechanical flaying machines has also resulted in the death of many trees. By their very nature, the Levels are short of tree nest sites, and so the holes and fissures in the trees that do exist are very important to wrens and little owls.

REED WARBLER

Summer on the Levels is underscored with the calls from this summer visitor. However, while the reedbeds of the rhynes (traditional drainage channels) reverberate to its whirring song, this skulking bird is seldom seen. In this area of dense reedswamp, vocal communication is more effective than visual signals, so exposure becomes a worthless risk. Between mid April and mid June a deep cylindrical cup of woven grass stems is lined with wool and feathers. These nests, built over water, usually bind together young reedstems, and the whole structure rises as the reeds grow. Four eggs are incubated by both birds for eleven to twelve days, and the chicks are fed by the pair for a further thirteen while they remain in the nest. These birds are reliant on the lifecycle of aquatic insects and thus never breed far from water.

KINGFISHER

Throughout the Somerset Levels kingfishers can be seen fishing from favoured branches that overhang larger drainage channels and canalized rivers. In recent times there has been concern that the clearance of traditionally pollarded willows has robbed them of suitable vantage points. Though at times plentiful, kingfishers have been given special protection due to their seasonal vulnerability. While, like the dipper, their aquatic feeding habits generally protect them from winter food shortages, a hard winter with prolonged freezing can cause thousands to starve. In April kingfishers search for nest sites, favouring overhanging river banks with soft soil, though some nests are some distance from water. Both birds will excavate an egg chamber between one and three feet long, a task that may take over a week. Six to seven eggs are incubated by both birds for about twenty days, and chicks are tended for a further twenty-five.

COWSLIPS

Cowslips were once commonplace, but the last twenty years has witnessed their sad decline. The move from traditional haymaking to silage production has resulted in much earlier cutting, destroying wild flowers before they have a chance to seed. Even where haymaking is still practised, the increased use of nitrogen has produced lush strong grasses that strangle the uncompetitive cowslip. Today many areas of the Somerset Levels are designated ESAs (Environmentally Sensitive Areas). With cash inducements to farm more traditionally, the cowslip is making a comeback. These were photographed on the banks of the River Brue. The adjoining meadow was full of cowslips, lady's smock, buttercups and daisies — nothing rare, but beautiful to look at.

WITHY CUTTING

The withy industry has been a feature of the Levels since man moved into the area. Twelve-inch canes are pushed into the wet ground and harvested two to three years later. Baskets and cane furniture are still produced locally.

RHYNES

As this great wetland has shrunk, the rhynes of the area have provided a reservoir or bolt hole for the aquatic plants and animals. Because of this, sensitive management is essential. Though they must be cleaned regularly (every two to five years), care should be taken to leave undisturbed areas so that plants and animals can migrate to unspoilt waters when the time suits them. The method of clearance is also of prime importance: if mechanical methods are used, care must be taken not to damage the bottom or sides of the ditch. Lastly, rhynes must be protected from farm effluent, such as slurry. With good maintenance, ditches can encourage species like otter, dragonfly and kingfisher.

COTTON GRASS

Peat cutting and land drainage have severely restricted this water-loving plant, but it can be found on the few remaining peatland areas of the Levels. The filaments that make up the cotton head start out as short hairs around the ovary. After the flowers have been fertilized the hairs lengthen and the whole plant becomes recognizable. In common with many sedges, the low sugar and starch content of the cotton grass protect it from grazing cattle, allowing it to enliven the aspect of the poorer dairy pasture on the Levels. In the past the fluffy heads were used in the production of candlewicks and are still used as stuffing for pillows and mattresses. It is seen at its best in June and July.

GREAT DIVING BEETLE

This voracious carnivore is fairly common in the ponds and rhynes of the Levels. Though well adapted to an aquatic existence, there are some telltale signs of its terrestrial history. For instance, the insect has no gills, and so it must periodically return to the surface and push the rear of its abdomen into the air; at the same time, the wing covers are lifted and thus air is trapped underneath them. The larval stage of the beetle faces the same respiratory problems, and so it, too, upends to breathe. Furthermore the larva must gain dry land to pupate. The eggs are deposited on waterplants during the summer. When full grown, the larvae are 3 cm long and even more rapacious than their parents: they will attack and eat almost anything that moves. Pupae emerge at any time from July to October, and the parents are present in all months except December and January.

WATER VOLE

Anyone walking beside a rhyne on a summer's day is almost bound to hear the characteristic 'plop' of the diving water vole. This creature is superbly adapted to an aquatic existence and swims and dives readily. It is also firmly rooted near the bottom of the food chain, eaten by hawks, owls, otters, stoats, weasels, mink, foxes, herons and any other predator large enough to get their mouth round it. Because of this, it prefers well-vegetated banks hosting the grasses and sedges that form the bulk of its diet. Though generally vegetarians, there is some evidence that they will take carrion. The breeding season begins in March, with the first litters born in April. The breeding chamber of closely woven rushes is usually below ground, and here four to six young are weaned by two weeks.

GRASS SNAKE

Though the grass snake is the least aquatic of Europe's three water snakes, it is an excellent swimmer and readily exploits the abundant aquatic prey species, like frogs, newts and toads. The village pond where this specimen is seen hunting was to become a car park for canal-side tourists. Whether or not this plan came to fruition, it is indicative of the pressure that pond habitats are under. Grass snakes are active from April to October, the rest of the year being spent in hibernation under tree roots or in a sand bank. They mate soon after waking and thirty to forty eggs are laid in July. As with most snakes, incubation is achieved through the warmth of the surroundings, and so compost heaps and other warm areas are favoured. About six weeks later the eggs hatch, revealing snakes about seven inches long.

COMMON TOAD

During the nights in early spring countless toads are crushed by cars as they migrate between hibernation sites and the clay pits and rhynes where they mate. Their breeding behaviour is similar to that of the common frog, except that toad spawn, which trails behind the pair in long dark strings, is wound around underground vegetation. Toad gatherings often number hundreds, and if females are outnumbered scores of males may attempt to mate the same female, creating a 'toad ball' and drowning the female. Such concentrations of animals obviously attract predators, and this early season bounty is tremendously important. Once the adults have left the water, the larvae of amphibian species become prey to dragonfly and damselfly nymphs.

FLOODED PEAT WORKINGS

Local conservation groups manage flooded peat workings in Somerset in the hope of recreating the best aspects of the Norfolk Broads. Old peat workings reveal the clay deposits laid down by the sea 6,000 years ago. In this period (before peat was laid down) the area was reedswamp, and this habitat returns when the peat has been removed. Though reedswamp is a valuable habitat (marsh harrier and bittern have visited recently), so too is southern raised peat bog.

PEAT CUTTING

There is precious little raised peat bog left on the Somerset Levels, and the last remnants look set to disappear. Originally these areas supported sphagnums, pale butterwort, the lesser butterfly orchid and other bog inhabitants, but these plants are unable to withstand the disruption and drainage inflicted by peat cutting. Originally this exploitation was a small scale operation, but the domestic market for compost now justifies a more systematic approach.

GREAT CRESTED GREBE

The anaerobic conditions of the Levels create quality clays that were once used in brick and tile making. As these industries died out, the pits were filled with water and became nesting grounds for many wildfowl, including the great crested grebe. This bird was so persecuted for its skin, that it was reduced to just fifty pairs in 1860. However, helped by the creation of artificial wetlands, its numbers have now reached relative safety. The rituals of mating, involving a complicated mirroring of each other's behaviour, is famous and spectacular. In recent years they have also taken to breeding in the flooded peat workings. From May to July, aquatic plants and vegetable detritus are shaped into the nest. These are often floating structures, secured to reeds or other vegetation. Three to six eggs are incubated by both birds for a period of twenty-five to twenty-nine days. The hatchlings stay with the adults for up to twelve weeks.

WHITETHROAT

Though not entirely a bird of the wetlands, the whitethroat is often found in woodland copse and hedgerows adjacent to water. On the Levels it nests in small woodlands and hedgerows left by less intensive dairy farming. These havens are rich in the insects needed for successful breeding. Whitethroats are summer visitors, arriving in April from sub-Saharan Africa, and departing in September. Early May sees four to five eggs laid in a deep, loosely built cup. The nest is largely built by the male before he has found his mate, but she will line it with plants, down and wool. Both sexes incubate for at least eleven days and the chicks remain in the nest for a further ten days. Though they are fairly common now, a drought in their wintering grounds killed 80% of the British breeding population in 1969.

LAPWING

The lapwing, or pewit, is a constant emblem of the Levels, and along with the red-shank is the most common breeding wader. Both species are present all year round and can be found feeding on the nearby Severn Estuary. Lapwing move to their breeding grounds in March and the first clutches are laid in early April. Incubation is by both sexes for about twenty-six days. As with all wader chicks, the young are mobile from the first day, though they are brooded for the next week or so. It is during this period that a high water table in marshland areas is so vital, for if it falls the invertebrates that make up the lapwing diet will sink with it.

THE BLACK DARTER

This dragonfly is something of a rarity on the Levels, though the remaining peaty ditches and streams support local populations. Mature males of this species are almost entirely black but for the lemon yellow on the upper part of the head. Females are predominantly black and yellow, ageing to ochre yellow. In Britain the species overwinters as eggs, and the larvae mature the following year emerging from the water to pupate in August. The adults are then on the wing until September. The males hover over boggy areas while the females hide themselves amongst heather and grasses. As soon as females venture over open water they are approached by, and soon paired with, a male. Mating takes place on nearby vegetation. The female lays the eggs alone, slapping the surface of the water with her abdomen, and then returns to the security of nearby vegetation.

Cuckoo Flower
(Lady's-Smock)

This is a plant of damp pastures and streamsides. On the Levels it grows prolifically on dairyland, and, being an early-flowering species (from April to May), it is unaffected by early cutting for silage. According to folklore, the cuckoo flower has sinister powers, such as increasing the chance of snakebite if picked, or encouraging lightning to strike any house it has entered. The lower leaves are similar to watercress, and may be eaten in the same manner.

MARSH MARIGOLD

The marsh marigold blooms
as early as March on the
Levels, bringing a brilliant
golden colour to the banks of
the rhynes early in the season.
It is another plant that loves
damp places and its large
flowers attract many insects.
In the past it was used to ward
off fairies and witches. The
local name 'king cup' is
evidently derived from its
resemblance to a King's
golden buttons ('cup' being
an evolution of 'cop',
meaning button).

CRESTED NEWT

Adult crested newts shelter from winter frosts in tree crevices and under stones that surround their breeding ponds. In spring they leave these places and move to the water, preferably deep weedy pools (the decline of traditional ponds seems to have hit this species harder than other amphibians). The male grows a toothed crest along his back with a mother-of-pearl stripe on the sides of the tail. The female has no vertebral crest, though there are tail ridges. During mating the male deposits a bundle of sperm which the female takes into her cloacal chamber. Here the eggs are fertilized before being attached individually to aquatic plants. The mating garb of the adults fades, and in autumn they leave the pond. The tadpoles hatch in about three weeks, and will mature in about ten.

COMMON NEWT

This young common newt has just left the water. Common newts are largely terrestrial, spending their days under stones and hunting for invertebrates, but they must return to water to breed. In spring they arrive at ponds, ditches and slow-moving rivers, where after a short mating ritual the male releases sperm which the female takes into her body. The fertilized eggs are attached individually to rocks and plants. Newt tadpoles breathe with the aid of feathery gills which protrude from the side of the head; these will persist until the larvae are mature in August. Late-maturing larvae may overwinter in this condition. Most young newts will become prey for grass snakes, birds and larger amphibians.

EUROPEAN COMMON FROG

The Somerset Levels plays host to just this native species of frog. As with other amphibians, the end of hibernation (February for frogs) is the cue for mating. To breed, frogs return to the place of their own spawning (even if it has been filled); the males first, closely followed by the females. Here, once paired, the male cleaves to the female's back and fertilizes the 1,000–2,000 eggs. These hatch in about two weeks, and the tadpoles leave the water when they are perfect miniatures of the adult. Both tadpoles and froglets are important prey items for water beetles, grass snakes and other predators. Nationally, the number of frogs has fallen due to the widespread use of pesticides and the substitution of drinking troughs for meadow ponds.

CANADA GEESE

Though this species was introduced only 250 years ago, Somerset's open water and good grazing have made it a common bird on the Levels. Approach the nest and it cranes its head forward, always looking directly at you full of menace. The nest is usually located on an island in a lake, as this one is, and hidden in some wooded area. In late May/early June a depression in the ground is lined with plant material and down, then an average of five eggs are incubated by the female alone. The chicks are mobile shortly after hatching, though they are tended by both parents for a further nine weeks until they can fly, and will remain with their parents until next season.

• WOODLAND •

BLUEBELL WOOD

The classic vision of spring in a British woodland must contain bluebells. The bulbs have in the past been used for glue and as a source of starch for the elaborate Elizabethan ruffs. Living in such a light restricted environment, the plant is very dependent on its leaves for photosynthesis. In fact, by growing larger leaves, it can adjust to light levels that would kill most plants. Because of this, the trampling of bluebell leaves will starve the plant, whereas the picking of its flowers does little damage. This picture was taken in young beechwood on the Quantock Hills in Somerset.

TURN BACK THE clock 6,600 years. The Ice Age has finally left Britain; massive landforms of melting ice still feed swollen rivers and large meltwater lakes. Indeed, much of lowland Britain is submerged under encroaching sea or freshwater. Most dry land is covered with trees – but this forest is new.

The ice's retreat began in 12000 BC as the age of arctic tundra passed. Species of tree swept over Britain in a procession dictated by changes in climate. From the south, birch, sallow and aspen were first to take advantage. By 8500 BC pine and hazel replaced the colonizing birch, to be followed by oak and hazel which dominated in the north and west, while lime did the same in the south and east; hardy pine and birch colonized the central and eastern Highlands. This was the great British wildwood.

Around 1000 years BC, man made his first substantial inroad into the wildwood with the clearance of the fertile alluvial soils of the Somerset Levels and East Anglia. The lime tree's affinity for good lowland soil made it the first target for clearance, but by the Bronze Age agricultural clearance had reached the uplands. By 500 BC, 50% of the wildwood was gone and much of today's farmland had been established. This spread of agriculture was necessitated by the growth in population; by the mid-Roman period (fourth century), Britons numbered 5 million. The next 200 years saw the only substantial rise in woodland since the post-glacial period. The Black Death had scythed the population to 1.5 million by the sixth century, and the prized farmland in Roman Essex reverted to the third largest wood of Domesday Britain. But apart from this respite deforestation was inexorable. In the 800 years following Domesday, woodland declined by two-thirds while the population doubled in less than 200 years. The fens were redrained and the weald turned over to farmland; Domesday woodland was lost at the rate of 20 acres a day. What remained was used very intensively. Indeed, from the sixth century, woodlands in the south became a managed resource. From as early as 500 BC man practised coppicing, and until the mid-nineteenth century woodland remained integral to his social and economic way of life. These woods would have jarred our visions of an idyllic rural past. Today woodland is a byword for 'natural' or 'unspoilt', but up until the middle of the last century woodland management was more akin to factory farming. A felling rotation of five to seven years produced poles for fencing and wattle and daub. A few 'standard' oaks were left for seventy years to provide special building timbers, but these were a rarity: in a world without power tools, the toil of working bulky lumps of hardwood was prohibitive. The forest was much sought after for many other domestic uses, and all rights to gather wood for burning, to graze pigs and even to gather leaves were audited and controlled. In this climate, woodland was prized and nurtured and its creatures flourished.

If the history of British woodland depicts a battle with agriculture, then this system of woodland cultivation could at least hold its own. During the population explosion of the Middle Ages woodland was coppiced so intensively that the monks of Bury St Edmunds had to search 250 miles for large oaks, and many of the great panels found in churches dating from this period were imported from the Continent. Again in the seventeenth century the agrarian revolution put land use under great scrutiny, but the income that forests produced plus the cost of clearance saved most woodland. In fact, there could never be any doubt that the prime producer of building material, animal fodder and fuel would survive: its products were the mainstay of English society.

The death knell for British woodland was not felling at all, but the decline of the market for woodland crops. By 1850 crops such as coppice poles and timber no longer came from British woodland. According to Oliver Rackham, 'Britain got into the habit of obtaining its cellulose by plundering other countries' wildwood.' When this practice was interrupted by German U-boats, it was decided that Britain should grow her own. Unfortunately the skills of woodland conservation appeared piecemeal and inefficient to modern thinkers who quickly replaced ancient woodland with exotic conifers. Though the latter appear to be a more cost-effective crop, the new plantations are an inhospitable desert for wildlife.

Deciduous woodland will support higher densities of animals than almost any other habitat. The variety of this ecology is due, in part, to the good cover afforded by the foliage, but the ability of trees to pull nutrients from deep in the soil and make them available to smaller plants and animals also maintains the richness of the environment. Spring in broad-leaved woodland finds plants of the understorey making the most of sunshine that will be obscured by the leaves of high summer. Their colours and scents spur insects into life, and this in turn fuels the early summer of many small mammals such as shrews and dormice. In contrast, the permanent gloom of the conifer plantation permits few flowers and insects. This distinction continues throughout the year, ending in broad-leaved woodland's autumn bounty corresponding to a conifer plantation's seed crop that few native species can use. Tragically, the thirty years after 1945 saw 50% of existing ancient woodland given over to afforestation. We had destroyed in twenty-eight years what had survived the last 800.

The generally low levels of wildlife found in these new bleak monocultures indicate that many species experience difficulties. Bats, for instance, are discouraged by the low number of insect species, as are the host of warblers and song birds of Britain's native woodland. The leaf litter creates a soil so acid that where light does penetrate, the range of understorey plants is severely limited. While animals may speak for wildlife's preference for variety, voices should also be raised in the interests of people. Most would prefer a natural woodland, given the choice. But if history has taught us anything, it is that having controlled our own environment, we get the woodland we deserve. For example, the woodland of the 1770s was appropriate to its times. Its importance to the people insured its health, and the uses it was put to created its variety. Unfortunately, most of today's woodland is also appropriate for its time. As woodland management now follows the logic of arable farming, it is not surprising that the crop looks and is harvested like wheat.

In only one location can we catch a glimpse of the original wildwood. Remote from large populations and often on soils too poor to tempt the farmers axe, the Caledonian Forest lets us 'taste' the past.

THE CALEDONIAN FOREST

Six thousand years ago this forest covered most of central Scotland. Today the forests of Abernethy, Rothiemurchus, Glen Mor and Inshriach/Invereshie are remaining pockets distributed across Speyside. Though these constitute the largest area of semi-natural woodland in Britain it is less than 1% of the original Caledonian wildwood. From the heights of Graig Fhiaclach (Britain's only natural upper tree line), down the slopes of the Cairngorms to the forests and lochs of Abernethy, the Highlands show the Scots pine at its best, but the wildwood also has rowan, alder, aspen and birch on the more fertile soils at the forest edge.

It is the forest's understorey that first captures the imagination; the ancient trees sparsely mixed with heathers and lichens seem rich and primeval. Where the forest is more dense, bilberry and cowberry provide food for capercaillie chicks, and damper areas reveal lush green carpets of moss. Plants from post-glacial Britain, Boreal relics from 8,000 years ago can still be found here: St Olaf candlesticks; twin flower; and the orchids, lesser twayblade and creeping ladies tresses.

Early morning in winter and spring are the best times to see red deer browsing in this understorey. Roe deer are also a common sight as they stroll between juniper scrub on their way to daytime resting areas. But I suppose if any creature characterizes the Scottish pinewoods, it is the red squirrel. This species, once common throughout Britain, finds its last stronghold in these woods. In truth, red squirrels were a species of conifer woodlands, left stranded in England's broad leaved woodland by a change in climate. As soon as a real broad-leaved specialist arrived in the shape of the grey squirrel, they were out-competed.

Mammalian predators of Caledonia suffered the same persecution as those throughout Britain; maybe even more so here, where the protection of grousemoor has been an obsession. Wild cats and pine martin have hung on but you will be very lucky to see them; the same is true of the otter that inhabits the lochs and streams.

The bird life of the area is spectacular. Golden eagle and osprey attract most bird watchers, but there are other distinctive species. The forest lochans have tempted breeding goldeneye from Scandinavia, while Scottish crossbills are unique to these pinewoods. Crested tits are found elsewhere in Europe, but the entire British population relies on these woods. They often nest on the upper limit of the forest where bilberry gives way to heather. These areas are full of the bleached and broken bones of dead pines, and though they prove popular nesting sites for tits, they are a stark reminder of the fate that awaits this forest unless something is done.

The problem is overgrazing. As fast as seedlings become established, sheep, deer and rabbits eat them. In many areas the youngest tree is 100 years old and the oldest over 300. Unless grazing by red deer is curtailed, the forest will die of old age. The danger of overgrazing was first reported at the beginning of this century and while the 'red deer problem' has been talked about *ad infinitum*, it has only been damage to agriculture that has been addressed.

Ironically, deer were all but extinct in the Highlands by the eleventh century. In fact, hunting had eradicated most large mammals from Scotland 800 years ago (the moose in the tenth century, bear in the eleventh and the reindeer in the twelfth). Rescue for the red deer began with the same feudal hunting restrictions that created the New Forest, but, none the less, by the mid-eighteenth century deer were restricted to a few areas to the north of the great fault. Their recovery arrived with the nineteenth century's obsession with deer stalking, and the subsequent establishment of deer forests at Mar and Atholl in the Grampians. With the decline in profitability of sheep farming, country pursuits became the thing. Huge herds of hinds were kept to entice stags onto estates, and deer numbers grew. Though this period developed a code for hunting, it failed to produce a system of management based on the ecology of the quarry.

With the exception of wartime premiums on fresh meat (venison was not rationed, especially if it was poached), deer numbers rose. In 1960 they numbered 150,000, by

THE CALEDONIAN PINEWOODS

This picture looks south over Rothiemurchus to the peaks of Carn Eilrig and Cairn Odhar. Though pine trees grow all over Britain, varying in size and shape with the prevailing conditions Rothiemurchus seems to show them at their best. Despite the evergreen canopy, these natural woodlands permit sunlight to reach the forest floor and fuel a diverse woodland ecology. The forest understorey is rich, creating an abundant insect life. This in turn feeds the young of small birds, which themselves become food for mammalian predators. In the canopy the seed crop of this native species is eaten by squirrels and birds. Such interdependence does not occur in conifer plantations. This was a favoured early morning spot for roe deer and an excellent area to watch red squirrels.

1989 this had risen to 300,000, and where densities were once five deer per square kilometre they are now fifteen (the recommended density for regeneration is two per square kilometre). This, allied with the loss of wintering grounds to afforestation, has put excessive pressure on those forest areas that remain.

But what is the 'natural number' of deer? It is a tricky question. To say that the 'red deer problem' was caused by the annihilation of natural predators is not helpful. Likewise, asserting that deer numbers should be allowed to rise till they reach the habitat's natural carrying capacity would merely reduce the forest to grassland.

In recognition of the damage deer were doing to agriculture, the Red Deer Commission was established in 1959 with the general remit to protect crops and reduce the number of deer. Though it has managed the former, the red deer cull consistently falls below the annual increase in deer populations. Much of the culling is left to estates, and their reluctance to comply with the cull quota (required by the RDC) has two obvious motives. Firstly, the capital values placed on stags (£20,000–£40,000); secondly, culling is an expensive business for the 40% of estates that do not commercially let stalking.

For a time it was hoped that a market for venison might alleviate the problem. But the opening of Eastern Europe and therefore cheap venison has meant that Germany, previously Scotland's best market for venison, pays so little that venison could never become a basis for deer management. The grants provided for fencing have protected some areas, but the inhumanity of allowing beasts to starve has been graphically illustrated. Hundreds of deer have starved, pressed against a fence in an effort to reach the food that could save them.

As it is, over 90% of the native woodlands are in Scotland and most are unfenced and unmanaged. While the hunting fraternity abhor systematic attempts to reduce deer numbers, labelling them 'absolute slaughter', it seems this is the best way of attaining the government-stated aim of ensuring that 'deer do not exceed the capacity of the land to provide for them'. Two thirds of the red deer were thought to be superfluous in the 1950s, so one wonders what will be necessary today.

Protecting the Caledonian Forest is of profound importance. Britain has destroyed so much of her wildwood that these few remnants are the last chance for species like the wild cat, and the best habitat for others like the red squirrel. There was a time when our rural lifestyle produced a direct, commonplace experience of wildlife. For example, the nineteenth-century poet John Clare (probably in his way the first ecologist) tells us how the 'shepherds weather glass', or how scarlet pimpernel predicted storm or fair with the opening and closing of its petals. But we have long since lost this easy association with nature.

Brown Argus

This is the only member of the blue family to lack all blue coloration in both sexes. Though not a woodland species, this pair was photographed in a clearing in limestone woodland on the Mendips. The brown argus is generally common on southern chalk and limestone hills, where there are two generations, from May to June, and from August to September. In the north, however, it is confined to one generation, from July to August. The eggs are laid on the limestone-loving plant, rock rose, and the common storksbill. Larvae of the second generation will hibernate and feed again before the two week pupation.

A Ryde in Somerset Beechwoods

The woodland of the Quantocks was reputedly one of Samuel Taylor Coleridge's favourite haunts. If true, then he may have witnessed their transition from managed woodland to the stand of 'natural' trees shown in this picture. Clues to its more manicured past can be seen in the picture opposite. Within the woods, the ryde edges are banked, and hedges that have not been coppiced for two hundred years now appear no more than a line of trees. Deciduous woodland on limestone soils, like these, hosts a great diversity of flowering plants and insects. This richness presents opportunities for more species of birds, mammals and insects than any other habitat.

FOREST BUG (SHIELD BUG)

These insects are found mainly in oak and hazel trees whose leaves form the bulk of their diet, although in spring they will consume any caterpillars they come across. Overwintering as nymphs in nooks and crannies of the canopy they constitute a valuable source of winter food for birds, especially tits. It is this type of variety in food supply at times when food is at a premium that makes deciduous woodland such a rich environment.

THE CRESTED TIT

This is one of the few species than can colonize forestry plantation, if only on the margins of older stands. They have two further requirements in order to make use of this habitat: firstly nest boxes are needed to replace favoured nest sites in the dead trees; secondly, crested tits must have access to mature stands of heather which provide winter shelter and food. All in all, most crested tits rely on the native woodlands of the central and eastern Highlands of Scotland where the abundance of summer insects allows the bird to thrive. Their breeding season begins in April/May when four to six eggs are laid in a hole excavated in rotten wood. The female is then fed by the male for the next fifteen days as she incubates the eggs. The young are then tended by both parents for the next twenty days.

BLACKCAP

This highly arboreal warbler exhibits a preference for broad-leaved woodland. It is most often seen singing or foraging in the canopy. Though the blackcap's nest site is often in low bushes or rank vegetation, its chicks are fed with insects gleaned primarily from woodland. The breeding season begins in late May, soon after the birds have arrived from their wintering grounds in Africa. The nest is a neat cup of grasses, lined with down and moss. Usually five eggs are laid and incubation is by both birds. The eggs hatch after twelve days and the chicks are tended by both parents for a further two weeks. A few birds winter in the south-west of Britain and, for these, fruits and the larvae of, for example, shield bugs are vital.

CALEDONIAN BIRCH WOODS

These woods occur on the more fertile edges of the conifer forest, or on the wetter valley bottoms. They have their own flora and fauna, such as the Kentish glory moth found in the woodlands above Braemar. This moth was once common throughout Britain, but it is now probably extinct in England. Birch trees have the ability to grow on thin soil, and such woods on block scree produce prime wildcat territory. Tree pipits, willow warblers and buzzards are typical of the nesting birds in this woodland.

THE SICKENER (RUSSULA EMETICA)

An unprepossessing name for a common fungi of the Caledonian pinewoods. These poisonous, bright red mushrooms catch the eye at first, but in the Highlands one soon becomes accustomed to their striking appearance. They have a beechwood cousin, the beechwood sickener, which is also poisonous.

FLY AGARIC (AMANITA MUSCARIA)

Variable in both height and colour, the fly agaric may appear with the classic mushroom parasol and in any colour on a spectrum from yellow, through orange to red. The varying appearance of this poisonous fungi can lead to it being confused with the edible amanitas. It is frequently seen among the conifers of the Caledonian pinewoods, though it is also found elsewhere.

PRIMROSE

This 'first rose' of spring is a common signal that winter is really over. Flowering at a time when insects are scarce makes pollination difficult, but, when fertilized, the plants produce sticky seeds that are highly attractive to insects. Thus the inefficiencies of pollination are compensated by excellent dispersal. The primrose is native to woods, hedgebanks and grassy places, though overpicking has made it less common than it once was. In the Middle Ages, the primrose had numerous uses, including medicinal remedies for general aches and pains and even a love potion.

SWEET VIOLET

This native perennial is common among the woods and hedges of the south, especially those on calcareous soils, though it is rare in the north and Ireland. The sweet violet was used as an air freshener in times before sanitation. Along with its scent, the flowers emit ionine which quickly dulls the olfactory processes, thereby giving immunity to sixteenth-century plumbing. Like many plants of broad-leaved woodland, the sweet violet must flower early in the season (from February to April). The petals may be white.

DORMOUSE

This elusive small mammal is
an indicator of quality
woodland. In recent years
broad-leaved woodland has
made a comeback in Britain,
but dormice live at such low
densities and produce so few
young that it is hard for them
to colonize new areas. They
have a liking for deciduous
woodland with plenty of
young growth and shrubs.
The trees should have edible
seed, like hazel, beech or
sweet chestnut, and the
shrubs should host the insect
life so vital to dormice during
midsummer. Distrusting the
ground, they like woodland
dense enough to allow
foraging without touching the
forest floor, but light enough
to provide the flower and
blossom they need in spring.
These conditions only occur
in forest glades that represent
a tiny proportion of a forest's
area. Regrettably, as Britain
has now lost 75% of its forest,
this habitat is virtually
non-existent.

MUNTJAC (BARKING DEER)

This small attractive deer,
native to the southern
mountains of China, was
introduced to Britain in 1900.
Today it is established in
much of southern Britain as a
result of escapes from deer
parks (notably Woburn in
Bedfordshire). There is little
evidence that it causes
agricultural damage and its
feeding is generally restricted
to seedling browse. However,
a recent report claims that
woodland with high muntjac
densities in Kent has been
stripped of its understorey,
stopping regeneration and
wiping out birds and insects
reliant on the shrub layer. The
muntjac's love of cover makes
it one of the few creatures that
frequent fir plantations,
though it often leaves cover at
night to feed. Why it makes
the staccato calls that give it
its colloquial name is largely
unknown, though it is often
an alarm cry.

ROE DEER

The roe is indigenous to Britain, but although common in medieval times hunting had restricted it to the borders of Scotland by the eighteenth century. Most of the animals of the south are the progeny of introductions to East Anglia and Dorset. This animal was photographed browsing in juniper scrub in Rothiemurchus, so it possibly derives from true Scottish stock. They are species dependent on cover and occur in both conifer and broad-leaved woodland. In the south, their major browse is bramble, while in Scotland this is replaced by heather and conifers. To what extent these and other herbivores, apart from red deer, contribute to the defoliation of the semi-natural woodlands of Scotland is a matter of some heated discussion.

RED DEER STAG IN HIGHLAND BIRCHWOOD

This is the largest and most majestic survivor of ancient British wildlife. Red deer provoke endless arguments about their numbers and the need to cull. The problem is that their penchant for the new shoots of conifer trees has halted forest regeneration. For many reasons their numbers are now above what most authorities agree are sustainable in the Highland forests. The British race of this species is now confined to north-west England, Scotland and probably south-west Ireland. Other populations further south are thought to be feral hybrids.

JAY

A bird more often heard than seen, this is the most handsome representative of the family *Corvidae*. Feeding on tree seeds, fruit, insects and small mammals, their diet is well suited to a woodland habitat. There has been speculation that their habit of cashing acorns in the winter may promote tree growth, though the efficient location of their buried foodstuffs undermines this argument. With their love of acorns, it is not surprising that their highest densities occur in oak woods. In May, five or seven eggs are laid in a cup of twigs, stems and mud, lined with fine roots and hairs. Both sexes incubate, and after seventeen days hatching coincides with a time of plenty in the forest. The young leave the nest after twenty days, though family groups seem to remain together throughout the winter.

GREATER SPOTTED WOODPECKER

The Revd F. O. Morris, part of a Victorian movement obsessed with the scientific assimilation of nature, referred to this bird as the Woodnacker, a name that probably claims too much for its rough carpentry, for though the nest appears in sound wood, the tree is often soft somewhere above the entrance hole. They are synonymous with British woodland where their diet of wood-burrowing insects and larvae can be supplemented with tree seeds and fruit in poor seasons. In May, the male and female excavate the breeding chamber and seven eggs are laid. Both birds share the nineteen day incubation and the tending of the young for a further twenty-one days.

EARLY PURPLE ORCHID

From April to June the lime-rich woodlands of the Mendips exhibit early purple orchids in profusion. The purple spots on the leaves in the foreground (said to be the blood of Christ dripping from the cross) distinguish this plant from the green winged orchid. During the sixteenth century, when these woodlands saw intensive use, the early purple orchid was used as a love potion. The ancient Greeks were said to determine the sex of their child by eating the tubers: if the father ate them then a boy would result; consumption by potential mothers would ensure girls.

WOOD ANEMONE

This fairly common woodland plant is unable to move across unwooded areas to colonize new woodland. This makes it a useful indicator of ancient woods, though the plant may persist in cleared areas. Other signs of old woodland include dog mercury and an absence of ivy (excepting limestone areas). Some plants need the cycle of light and dark created by coppicing to fulfil their lifecycle, and a recommencement of this practice has led to the germination of wood spurge seeds that have waited 125 years. The white, pink or purple flowers of the wood anemone appear in March and have faded by May.

SILVER WASHED FRITILLARY

The most magnificent of all the fritillaries this is a creature of older woodlands in southern England and Wales where it decorates the rides and clearings. Though it feeds on bramble and thistle, its greenish eggs need to be laid in the crevices of trees (unique among British butterflies), oak preferably but other species of tree are used. The larvae will hibernate here until the following spring when they emerge and move to another woodland plant, the dog violet. The adults are on the wing from June until September.

NUTHATCH

As woodland matures it provides the perfect environment for hole-nesting species like the nuthatch. This is a species of southern broad-leaved woodland, favouring oak and beech. Its habit of precluding predators by partially blocking nest holes with mud has led to the local name 'mudtopper', while the derivation of the beautifully descriptive 'nutjobber' and 'nuthacker' speak for themselves; it also feeds on larvae dug from soft wood. The six to nine eggs are laid in April or May and are incubated by the female for about two weeks. All the while, the male is feeding her and himself from the rapidly expanding insect population. If the insects are plentiful, then a second brood may be raised.

GREY SQUIRREL

Throughout England the grey squirrel has now all but replaced the red. The grey's more efficient feeding strategies and higher densities make it better adapted for life in broad-leaved woodland. However, red squirrels could live in forestry plantations if a few alterations were made to management practices: firstly, if selective felling replaced clear felling, then the disruption of harvest would be minimized; secondly, some trees must be allowed to mature – at present managed conifers are felled just as they reach maximum food production for red squirrels.

HEDGEHOG

The hedgehog inhabits the deciduous woodland and Mediterranean zones of western Europe. In Britain it is essentially a creature of the woodland edge, where it converges with grassland. Like the fox, it will leave daytime cover to feed in grasslands. The hedgehog's food is almost entirely ground-level invertebrates; caterpillars and beetles seem to be especially favoured, followed by earthworms and slugs. In season, bird's eggs and chicks will not be refused and this has led to the traditional persecution of this animal in the pursuit of game husbandry. In reality its diet makes it a useful ally for horticulturists. Hedgehogs hibernate from October till April in hibernation nests, and mating takes place soon after waking. Average litters of five young are born throughout the summer in specially constructed nest chambers, which will be changed if the mother is disturbed.

CALEDONIAN FOREST FLOOR

'The verdurous glooms and winding mossy ways' (Keats) of the closed forest seems to make the air taste of cool water. On the drier forest floors, bilberry and the lichen *Caledonia portentosa* (right) form a rich carpet that seems to cover and digest the discarded limbs of trees. Lichens, the symbiosis of algae and fungi, are abundant throughout these forests, hanging from every tree and sometimes covering the forest floor.

MOONLIGHT THROUGH THE PINES

'To stand in these woods is to feel the past,' said Steven and Carlise in a classic study of the area in 1959. At night, when fox, owl and otter are calling, the atmosphere is even more haunting. As dusk falls, the whistles of 'rodding' woodcock prelude the arrival of long-eared and pipistrelle bats. Deer and foxes leave cover to feed in open areas under cover of night, raising alarm calls from plovers nesting on nearby moorlands. For a nature lover, these woods seem full of timeless excitements.

FOX CUB

The fox has been persecuted more widely than any other predator, and since Elizabethan times there has been a reward for its corpse. Ironically there is little evidence that hunting in the traditional manner has any effect on population densities, but the maintenance of hunting covers has successfully protected woodland and scrub habitat from farming. Though their distribution ranges from 4,300-foot peaks in the Cairngorms to the centre of large cities, they are most often seen hunting earthworms and field voles on argricultural land, close to the woodland cover where they rest. This preference for daytime cover has brought them to the dense conifer plantations on moorlands, resulting in the disastrous predation of adjacent ground-nesting birds.

BADGER

This particular animal is part
of a group I have watched for
over ten years. The well-worn
path in the foreground
indicates regular use, though
this particular set is only fully
inhabited during the breeding
season. There are sets in
ancient woodlands near
Taunton that have been used
for at least three generations
of landowners. Badgers need
adequate cover, dry easily dug
soil, a plentiful food supply
that lasts all year, and
freedom from interference by
man or his animals. Though
badgers can live in a number
of habitats, their needs are
best met by deciduous
woodland, and it is here that
you will find them in their
highest densities. Where
woodland adjoins farmland,
the perceived threat to stock
(through bovine TB), poultry,
and the ruin of cereals has
caused persecution.

COMMON SHREW

These tiny mammals spend
their short lives (twelve
months) searching through
leaf litter for ground-level
invertebrates. Shrews born
the previous autumn mature
in spring and mate from
spring onwards.
Consequently young are born
anytime between May and
September. The female
constructs a domed breeding
chamber in a burrow or under
a log and inside this nest the
young are raised, becoming
independent in only
twenty-eight days. The female
will mate again almost
immediately and may raise
three broods a year. This
creature plays an important
role as a prey for species such
as barn owls. Shrews and
other small mammals are an
important pathway for the
produce of the forest to find
its way into the stomachs of
the carnivores. In autumn
many animals prepare for the
meagre rations of winter; the
combination of young and
old generations of small
mammals at this time provide
vital food for predators.

INDEX

BIBLIOGRAPHY

Bannerman, D. A., *Birds of the British Isles*, Oliver & Boyd, Edinburgh 1960

Barnes, R. S. K., *Estuarine Biology*, Edward Arnold, London 1974

Bibby, C. J., 'Impacts of Agriculture on Upland Birds', *Ecological Change in the British Uplands*, ed. M. B. Usher, Blackwell Scientific, Oxford 1988

Birks, H. J., 'Long Term Ecological Change in the British Uplands', *Ecological Change in the British Uplands*, ed. Usher, Blackwell Scientific, Oxford 1988

Blamey, Marjorie & Fitter, Richard S. R., *Wild Flowers of Britain and Northern Europe*, Collins, London 1974

Burton, John, *Oxford Book of Insects*, OUP, Oxford, 1968

Callander, Robin F. & Mackenzie, Neil A., *The Management of Wild Red Deer in Scotland*, Rural Forum Scotland, Perth 1991

Corbet, G. B. & Southern, H. N. (eds), *The Handbook of British Mammals*, Blackwell Scientific, Oxford 1964

Etherington, John R., *Wetland Ecology*, Edward Arnold, London 1983

Ferns, P. N., 'Birds of the Bristol Channel and Severn Estuary', *The Marine Pollution Bulletin*, ed. R. S. Glover, Pergamon, Oxford 1984, vol. 15, no. 2

Harrison, Colin, *Nest Eggs and Nestlings*, Collins, London 1975

Hulyer, ed., *The Severn Estuary: A Heritage of Wildlife*, The Severn Estuary Conservation Group, 1990

Kearton, R., *British Birds Nests and How to Identify Them*, Cassell, London 1895

Lindahl, Kai Curry, *The Future of the Cairngorms*, The North East Mountain Trust, 1982

McGeeney, Andrew, *British Dragonflies*, Cape, London 1986

Owens, Morlais, 'Severn Estuary: An Appraisal of Water Quality', *The Marine Pollution Bulletin*, ed. R. S. Glover, Pergamon, Oxford 1984, no. 2

Pearsall, W. H., *Mountains and Moorlands*, Collins, London 1950

Philips, Roger, *Wild Flowers of Britain*, Ward Lock, London 1977

Press, J. R., Sutton, D. A. & Tebbs, B. R., *Wild Flowers of Britain*, Readers Digest, London 1981

Putman, R. J., *Grazing in Temperate Ecosystems: Large Herbivores and the Ecology of the New Forest*, Croom Helm, Beckenham 1986

Rackham, Oliver, *Trees and Woodland in the British Landscape*, Dent, London 1990

Ratcliffe, D. A., 'Upland Birds and their Conservation', *British Wildlife*, vol. 2. no. 1, 1991

Ratcliffe, D. A. & Oswald, Philip, *The Flow Country*, The Nature Conservancy Council, 1988

Ratcliffe, D. A. & Thompson, D. B. A., 'The British Uplands: Their Ecological Character and International Significance', *Ecological Change in the Uplands*, ed. M. B. Usher, Blackwell Scientific, Oxford 1988

Steven, H. M. & Carlise, A., *The Pinewoods of Scotland*, Oliver & Boyd, Edinburgh 1959

Taylor, Kenny, 'Land Wildlife and Conservation in the Cairngorms', *British Wildlife*, vol. 2, no. 1, 1991

Tubbs, Colin, *The New Forest: An Ecological History*, David & Charles, Newton Abbott 1968

Tubbs, Colin, 'Grazing the Lowland Heaths', *British Wildlife*, vol. 2, no. 5, 1991

Warwick, R. M., 'The Benthic Ecology of the Bristol Channel', *The Marine Pollution Bulletin*, ed. R. S. Glover, Pergamon, Oxford 1984, vol. 15, no. 2

Williams, Michael, *The Draining of the Somerset Levels*, CUP, Cambridge 1970